MEASURE
TWICE
CUT
ONCE

MEASURE TWICE CUT ONCE

JIM TOLPIN

BETTER WAY BOOKS

Cincinnati, Ohio

To prevent accidents, keep safety in mind while you work. Use the safety guards installed on power equipment; they are for your protection. When working on power equipment, keep fingers away from saw blades, wear safety goggles to prevent injuries from flying wood chips and sawdust, wear headphones to protect your hearing, and consider installing a dust vacuum to reduce the amount of airborne sawdust in your woodshop. Don't wear loose clothing, such as neckties or shirts with loose sleeves, or jewelry, such as rings, necklaces or bracelets, when working on power equipment, and tie back long hair to prevent it from getting caught in your equipment. The author and editors who compiled this book have tried to make all the contents as accurate and correct as possible. Plans, illustrations, photographs and text have been carefully checked. All instructions, plans and projects should be carefully read, studied and understood before beginning construction. Due to the variability of local conditions, construction materials, skills levels, etc., neither the authors nor Betterway books assumes any responsibility for any accidents, injuries, damages or other losses incurred resulting from the material presented in this book.

Measure Twice, Cut Once. Copyright © 1993 by Jim Tolpin. Printed and bound in the United States of America. All rights reserved. No part of this book may be reproduced in any form or by any electronic or mechanical means including information storage and retrieval systems without permission in writing from the publisher, except by a reviewer, who may quote brief passages in a review. Published by Betterway Books, an imprint of F&W Publications, Inc., 1507 Dana Avenue, Cincinnati, Ohio 45207. 1-800-289-0963. First edition.

97 96 95 94 93   5 4 3 2 1

Library of Congress Cataloging in Publication Data

Tolpin, Jim
    Measure twice, cut once / by Jim Tolpin.
      p. cm.
    Includes bibliographic references (p. 115) and index
    ISBN 1-55870-305-5
    1. Woodwork — Amateurs' manuals.   I. Title
TT185.T64   1993
684'.08 — dc20
                                        93-22385
                                          CIP

Edited by Laura Tringali
Designed by Brian Roeth

Dedication

This book is for the kids in my life: Coyote Karrick, Isaac Tolpin, Jacob Middleton, Nathan Middleton and Yuri Tolpin-Bates. They measure up no matter how you cut it.

Acknowledgments

For lending me encouragement and a bit of their woodworking wisdom: Teri Mielke, Daniel Neville and David Lewis.

For lending a hand or a tool during the photo shoot: Jennifer Schwarz, Doug Warren, Isaac Tolpin, Charles Neu, Bob Kahne, Earnie Baird, Matrix Enterprises, Inc., The L.S. Starrett Co., Woodworker's Supply of New Mexico, Bridge City Tool Works, Veritas Tools, Inc. and Hitachi Tools, Inc.

And for her excellent editing skills (once again!):
Laura Tringali.

Table of Contents

Introduction

Chapter 1: *Concepts of Proportion and Measurement*

For those who do woodworking, and for those who enjoy the fruits of these labors, there exists a common sense of proportion and a common system of measurement. Understanding these basic elements of design and layout provides a woodworker with a firm foundation for creating beautiful, yet functional, pieces of furniture.

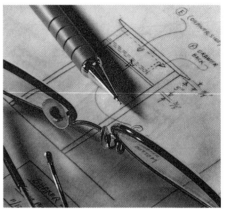

Chapter 2: *Drawing Techniques*

When preparing to build a piece of furniture you start by getting the design down on paper. Learning to have a free hand with concept sketches unleashes the creative instincts. Using the techniques of mechanical drawing, these ideas are then transformed into dimensioned and labeled working drawings.

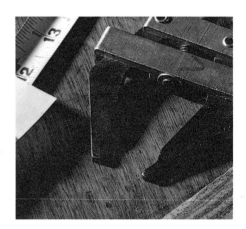

Chapter 3: *Creating Working Drawings and Cutlists*

Of the numerous ways to portray the form of an object on paper, woodworkers generally need only work with a few simple projections. Having created a scaled-down drawing of the project, the proportions and final dimensions are then confirmed in a full-scale rendering. By developing cutlists, templates and story poles from this rendering, a fail-safe bridge is formed between the paperwork and the woodwork.

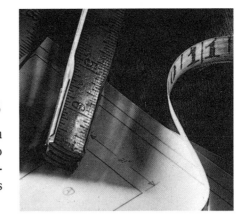

Introduction

"Measure twice, cut once." How often has this venerable expression echoed tauntingly through the sawdust-filled chamber between my ears? The truth is, countless times — as often as I've made critical cuts in very wrong places. I have to admit: If I had taken the time to measure twice, in all probability I would not be making the cut twice.

But I didn't write this book to drive home platitudes. I wrote it to help woodworkers learn to measure right the first time. To get the most out of your woodworking time, you must learn to lay out cutlines and assembly positions quickly and precisely. (While you are, of course, forever bound to checking your marks twice "for good measure," only rarely should you discover that a mark belongs somewhere else.) Although the various measuring and marking techniques I cover may at first glance seem daunting, I can assure you that layout is but another woodworking skill, a skill whose mastery is well within the reach of any woodworker.

This book begins with a discussion of the origins of our systems of measurement, concepts of proportion, and standards of furniture design. Please accept that learning about such things as *golden sections* and Vitruvius's exposition of human proportions is much more than an amusing glimpse into an esoteric world of ancient curiosities. I believe this knowledge to be basic information, wisdom really, that we woodworkers, wishing to become better woodworkers, should understand and respect. It makes little sense, after all, to take the time to lay out a complex piece of furniture, no matter how quickly and accurately, if it's going to come out dog-ugly and not be functionally fit for the people who will use it.

Achieving confidence that what you are going to build is worth building is your starting point. Knowing how to develop accurate and easy-to-follow working drawings and cutlists is the next important step. To help you take it, I'll introduce you to certain types of drawing projections and measurement scales that make the most sense for woodworkers planning the average furniture project. Then, from these working drawings, I'll show you how to create foolproof *picture board* cutlists. These sketches clearly indicate where to lay out the components on the stock in ways that maximize the beauty of the wood while minimizing waste.

But creating foolproof cutlists does not, on its own, ensure a perfectly cut pile of boards. You also need to master the tools and techniques that get the cutlists translated, without error, onto pieces of real wood. There is probably no greater agony for a woodworker than the discovery that the cut has just been made to the wrong side of a line or that an inch has irrevocably been lost due to the misreading of a tape measure. To these I would add the frustration of seeing a project "grow" in size if it is laid out from mark to mark, rather than laid out from a single reference point, or of discovering that an entire series of components has been misoriented and subsequently miscut.

Even if your layout is impeccable, however, there is still plenty of room for error in the cutting of the stock. Even very small deviations

from a desired crosscut angle can result in a structure not coming out square, or in the case of polygons, not coming together at all at the final joint. If the joints are not cut square to the face of the wood, the resulting assembly will not be flat—doors won't shut properly and drawers may bind. In addition, the overall size and shape of the structure may be off, causing problems when you assemble it to other components or attempt to fit it into an existing space. For these reasons, I feel it is as important to know the tools and techniques of cutting to the line as it is to know where and how to make the line in the first place.

Try as you may, and as skilled as you might become in the layout and cutting processes, mistakes will inevitably creep into any project. These probably occur just when the Goddess of Carpentry happens to be looking the other way (probably to watch the other guy make a real boner!). But having some neat tricks up your sleeve nearly always gives you a way out. Besides learning how to recut certain joints in unobtrusive ways, there are ways you can "stretch" the width and length of miscut boards. Defects and mis-drilled holes can be carefully patched so they'll be invisible to nearly everyone—except other readers of this book.

Of course, there is one mistake that proper design, layout and cutting skills may never prevent: making the project too big to fit through your shop door. You'll have to figure out that one for yourself!

Chapter 1

Concepts of Proportion and Measurement

M ost people to whom I've shown the table pictured at right don't like it. The table's proportions are decidedly disturbing. Many viewers tell me that the top is too thin, others point out that the horizontal board supporting the top is too thick and that the table is too squat. The "after" photograph shows the same basic table, only with a thickened top and reduced-size apron. Most viewers respond to it much more positively than the "before" design. When I built the revised design, I did not choose the new dimensions out of thin air. Instead I looked to the concepts of classical architecture to give me a sense of what constitutes ideal proportional relationships.

If I could show the "before" table to an influential Roman architect named Marcus Vitruvius Pollio (Vitruvius for short) of the first century B.C., it is highly probable that he would agree that its proportions are ungainly. Based on what is known about Vitruvius's study of ancient Greek and Egyptian rules of proportions, the thickness of the tabletop and apron relative to the overall dimensions of the piece are, quite simply, wrong. Another more widely known Italian architect (and a fan of Vitruvius), Leonardo da Vinci, would probably feel the same way. And in more recent times, so would the German school of architecture under Walter Gropius and the French school under Le Corbusier. So what did Vitruvius come up with? What is it about the proportions of the "before" table that just wouldn't seem right to these classical architects? To answer this question, we must take a short journey through the history of proportion.

According to the principles of classical architecture, the relative proportions of the top and the apron of this table are incorrect. As a result, most people find the design disquieting.

With a thicker top and a narrower apron, the table has been reproportioned to meet the visually pleasing ratio of the golden section.

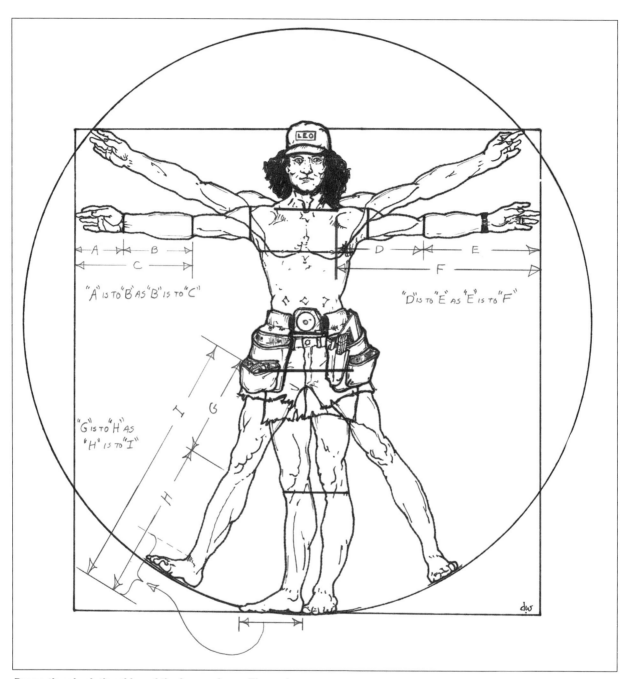

Proportional relationships of the human form. *The various portions of a person's body relate to one another in a simple ratio: The small portion is to the larger portion as the larger is to the sum of both.*

Adapted from da Vinci by Declan Westcott

Ancient Concepts of Idealized Proportions

Part of what Vitruvius discovered in his studies of ancient Greek and Egyptian theories of proportion was that these people recognized an incredible number of proportional relationships among the parts of a human body. He found, for example, that in the average person the foot is ⅙ the height of the body; the head is ⅛ and the hand ¹⁄₁₀. Man's center, the navel, occurs at ⅝ the total height.

Centuries after Vitruvius, Leonardo da Vinci used Vitruvius's observations to draw his famous figure of a man standing within a square and a circle. If you study the dimension lines in Declan Westcott's interpretation of da Vinci's drawing, at left, you'll see that the proportions of this woodworker's body parts relate to one another in a simple ratio. For example, the length of a hand is in proportion to the length of a forearm as the length of a forearm is in proportion to the sum of both. As you can see, this same ratio recurs throughout the body. Furthermore, it appears that this ratio also occurs throughout all of nature. Scholars have observed this particular proportional relationship in everything from the structure of spider webs and the swirl patterns of seed pods to the curve of a seashell's growth rings.

The Greeks, who were well aware of this ratio in the architecture of the ancient Egyptians, called this relationship the *golden section*. Its numerical ratio works out through analytical geometry to be about five to eight (contemplate the position of your navel for a moment, recalling that Vitruvius noted that it sits at ⅝ of your height).

From the beauty of the golden section, the Greeks derived a rectangle to express the ratio in the design elements of their temples. Studies of their works have shown that they always made their rectangles exactly 1.618 times longer than their width. The ancients didn't use direct measurements to lay out this golden rectangle, and there's no reason you need to either. All you need is a square and a compass. And once having drawn a golden rectangle, you can easily generate any number of others.

Now I can answer that question about what is wrong with the "before" table introduced at the beginning of this chapter. Its overall dimensions are based on the golden section, but the relationship of its internal elements is not. The thinness of the top is decidedly out of proportion with the massiveness of the supporting apron piece. In turn, the apron is out of proportion to the thickness of the legs. And while the height and width of the table creates a golden rectangle, the open space defined between the legs and under the apron piece does not.

In the "after" table, I have brought the thickness of the top, the height of the apron, and the width of the legs into proportion as defined by the golden section ratio. It is not a coincidence that the internal rectangle between the legs and apron also now defines a golden rectangle. To most eyes, this table is now a lot more pleasing to view.

As both ancient and contemporary schools of architecture have discovered, most people tend to be comfortable with design elements based on the golden section. In fact,

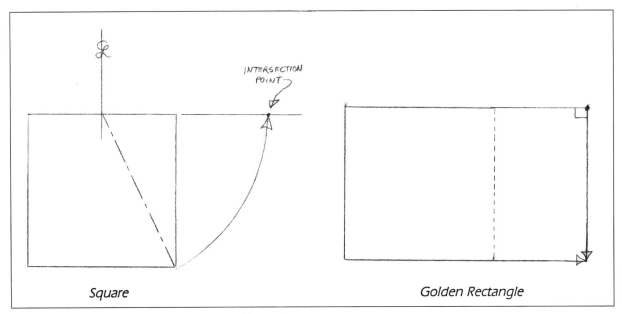

Square

Golden Rectangle

Using a compass and a square to create a golden rectangle. Step 1: *Swing an arc from the center point of the outside of a square form until the arc intersects the line extended out from the square.* **Step 2:** *Drop a line down at a 90° angle from the intersection point until it meets a line extended from the base of the square.*

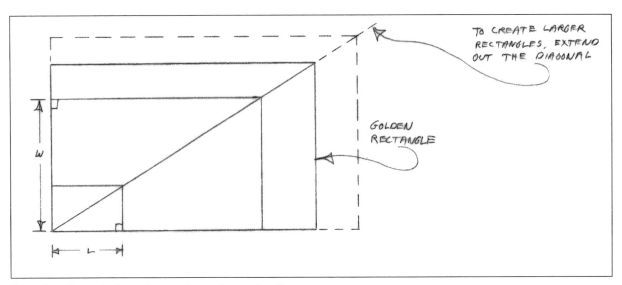

Using the diagonal of a golden rectangle to create others of varying sizes. *If you know the width, extend a line from here until it intersects the diagonal. Then drop a line at 90° to the base of the rectangle. If you know the length, extend the line up to the diagonal and then over to the side.*

rectangles based on the golden section exist not only in classical architecture, but in many everyday objects: from the shape of paper currency and plastic credit cards to the overall configuration of a Boeing 747. The French architect Le Corbusier felt that the expression of this ratio in the things we make for ourselves is a harmonious extension of our own bodies to the world around us. He used the golden rectangle to scale out everything in his structures from piazzas to bookshelves.

When Ideal Proportions Are Less Than Ideal

As you might suspect, however, all this emphasis on the "rightness" of the golden rectangle is a bit broadbrushed. The fact that the elements of an object have been designed around the golden section does not ensure that the overall structure will look attractive. Other factors of proportion often enter into the picture of what makes a design work. Sometimes, for example, it is necessary to deliberately make certain parts of the structure asymmetric in order to balance the whole.

In the accompanying photos, you'll note that the bottom rail of the frame and panel door is considerably wider than the top rail. The second view of this same door shows why it was made this way. Since the door belongs to a lower cabinet unit, the observer nearly always looks down at the door from above. Because of this perspective, the eye foreshortens the width of the lower rail. Building up the width of the lower rail fools the eye into believing the top and bottom rails are the same size.

A face-on view of this frame and panel lower cabinet door shows the bottom rail to be conspicuously wider than the top rail. Because this door is generally viewed from above, the asymmetry of the frame corrects the optical illusion that would otherwise make the bottom rail appear smaller than the top rail.

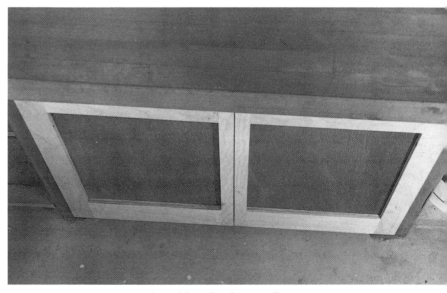

When viewed from above, the cabinet door's top rail appears about as wide as the bottom rail.

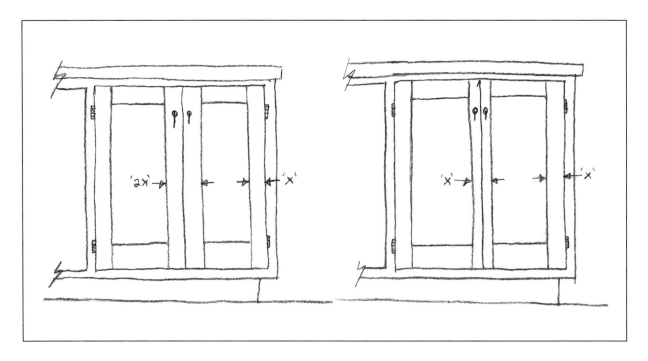

Using asymmetry to create more pleasing proportions. *The junction of the meeting stiles is double the width of a door stile. The reduced width of the meeting stiles in the drawing at right allows the junction to equal the width of one door stile.*

Another example of the use of asymmetry to balance proportions is illustrated in the drawing above. In the first view, the doors have stiles of equal size. When they are paired, the adjoining stiles visually read as one overwide (and thus poorly proportioned) stile. It is prudent, in this case, to reduce the size of the abutting individual stiles to balance the design.

Other Proportioning Systems

As appealing and as seemingly universal as the golden section is, there are a number of other ways to arrive at proportions that look right. You can use arithmetic, geometric or even Fibonacci series progressions to size everything from the graduated heights of drawer faces and stepped moldings to the overall dimensions of modular cabinets. Each of these systems share one thing in common with the golden section— consistency. The arithmetic pro-

gression adds a constant to each succeeding unit. The geometric maintains a constant ratio of increase, while the Fibonacci series builds upon the sum of the preceding two units. Like the proportions of the golden section, these progressions generally "feel" right to the eye.

A particularly attractive geometric progression—called the Hambridge progression—was developed in this century by the American scholar Jay Hambridge. With this system, it's extremely easy to develop nicely graduated drawer heights for a case front.

To generate the progression, first draw a square the width of the drawer face at the base of the scale drawing. Now set a large compass or trammel beam to the diagonal of the square and swing it up until it intersects the side of the case. This indicates the height of the first drawer face.

To find the height of the next drawer face, set the compass to the

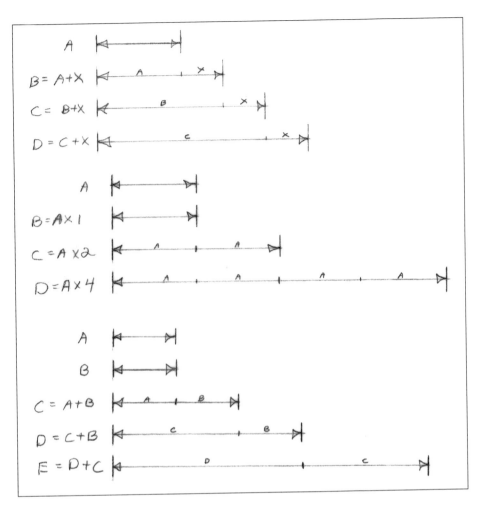

Examples of other types of proportional relationships. **Arithmetic progression:** *Each step exceeds the last by the addition of a constant (X) amount.*

Geometric progression: *The progression builds on a constant ratio. Here: x1, x2, x4, etc. You could also use x1, x3, x9 or any other constant ratio.*

Fibonacci series: *Each step (after the first two) is the sum of the preceding two units.*

diagonal from the same lower corner of the square to the opposite corner of the newly created rectangle. Swinging this line to the case side gives you the height of the next drawer. Continue until you have developed gradually smaller face heights for the number of drawers in the case. Note, however, that you cannot preset the total height of the case; it is a function of the number of drawers and the width of the case.

Architectural Graphic Standards

It is not enough, though, to proportion the elements of a piece of furniture to be in harmony with itself. It must also be properly proportioned to fit the purpose for which the furniture was made.

For nearly every object built for use, there is a standard height, depth and width that works best for most people. These figures are available in *Architectural Graphic Standards*, a reference book available in most public libraries. This book is updated regularly: Note that you won't find much about computer furniture in older versions. The chart lists standard measurements for some common furniture pieces. Use these as a starting point, adapting them as necessary to suit the intended user.

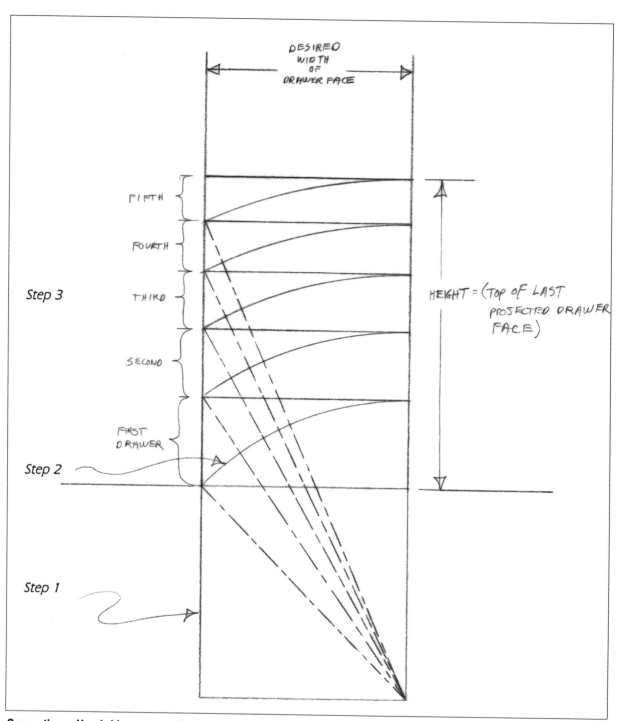

Generating a Hambridge progression. Step 1: *Construct the square under the drawer face.* **Step 2:** *Swing the diagonal of the square up to the side of the drawer face line.* **Step 3:** *Draw a horizontal line from the intersection of the arc with the side. Create a new diagonal and swing an arc to create the second drawer face height.*

Proportions of Common Furniture Pieces

Furniture	Width	Length	Height	Other Parameters
Dining Table	[allow 24″/person]		28-30″	25″ leg clearance between floor and apron
Children's Table	[allow 22″/child]		20-24″	Use with 13″ chair
Coffee Table	22-26″	36-60″	15-17″	
Computer Table	26-30″	36-60″	26″	Allow leg clearance at keyboard location
Writing Table	24-30″	30-48″	28-30″	25″ leg clearance
Dining Chair (seat dimensions)	18″	16″ (depth)	15-18″	Back forms 92°-94° angle with seat
Bookshelves	To suit	10-12″ (depth)	30-84″	Set appropriate shelf spacing, or use adjustable shelving
Kitchen work island	24-36″	48-72″	34-38″	If solid panels, provide toe kick
Beds	Add 2″ to size of mattress to determine width and length between sides and endboards			Top of mattress should be 12-16″ from floor

Concepts of Measurement

The other day out in my shop I cut a table leg to a height of 29¾″. There was nothing particularly unusual about this measurement, except for my sudden realization that it was totally arbitrary. A visiting woodworker from Switzerland was with me, and he pointed out that on his tape measure my table leg was 75.565 cm. Also a totally arbitrary number, I pointed out a little too smugly. In truth, the only thing concrete was the fact that this table leg was now just the right length to hold a plate of food in front of my face at just the right height. To explain where these numbers come from, I need to take you on a little tour through the history of measurement systems.

In the Old Testament of the Bible, one standard of measurement — the *cubit* — comes up again and again. Most notably, the cubit was the unit of measurement given by God to Noah to lay out the length and breadth of the great ark. An Egyptian standard of length known to exist as early as 3,000 B.C., the cubit is roughly the distance from your elbow to the tip of your index finger, about 20⅝″. It was, indeed, the arm of the great Sun God Pharaoh that established the cubit in

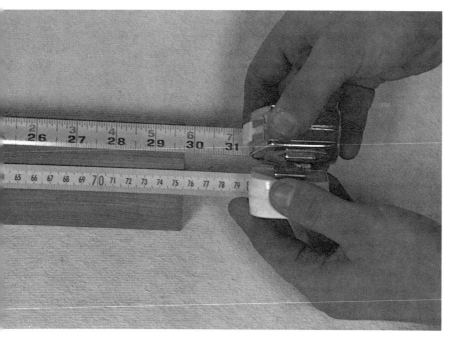

The length of this table leg is both 29¾″ in the English system of measurement and 75.565 centimeters in the metric system. While each measuring system has its advantages and disadvantages, my system of choice is no system at all — I avoid using numerical measurements whenever possible.

pace — a thousand paces then became one *mile*.

In later times, the artisans and merchants of England could be found still working with many of the measurement standards of the Egyptians and Romans. One exception stands out, however. It may have come about when some hefty Saxon noticed that twelve, rather than sixteen, of his own decidedly more chubby digits equaled the span of his foot. These finger widths were designated *inches*, with twelve in a row equaling a *foot*. The English went on to decide that three of these *feet* equaled a *yard*, and that the inch itself would be subdivided to equal three *barleycorns*.

To this day here in the United States, most people still use the linear measurement scale of the British Imperial System. Nearly everyone else on the planet uses a system of linear measurement based not on the sizes of human body parts and local vegetables but on a scientifically established standard of length. Initially, the *metric* standard of one *metre* (or meter) was mandated by Louis XVI of France to be the length of one ten-millionth of the total distance of a meridian line running between the earth's poles and passing through Paris, France. In more recent times, while our measurement forbearers were still fingering their feet, the standard length of the meter was fixed more precisely by equating its span to the wavelength of light generated by a hyperactive chunk of Krypton-86.

An essential distinction between the British Imperial System of measurement and the metric system (now referred to as the Systeme International, or S.I.) is immediately

the beginning. This length was cut into a slab of black granite, and all cubit sticks throughout the empire were regularly checked against this standard.

For work out in the field, the cubit was broken down into twenty-eight divisions called *digits* — the number of finger widths it took the Pharaoh to span from his elbow to his fingertip. For convenience, four finger widths were referred to as a *palm*; five were called a *hand*. Nothing too esoteric here, and nothing too shabby either. The largest pyramids built to this system met measurement tolerances of within five-hundredths of 1 percent over their entire breadth.

The Romans added a bit more to the Egyptian system, noticing that sixteen divisions of the Pharaoh's cubit equaled the length of a man's foot. The Romans, who did more than their share of marching about, also discovered that five foot-lengths made up an average person's

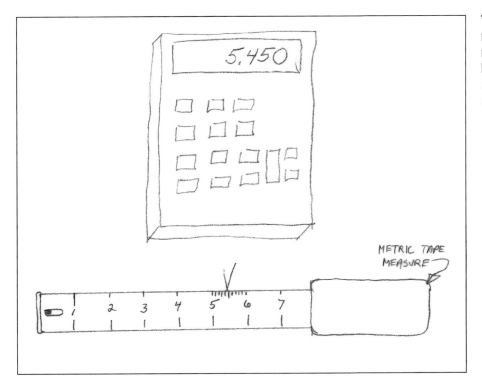

Transferring a calculator readout directly to the metric tape measure. To Calculate: *21.8 cm ÷ 4 = 5.45 cm. Then read 5.45 cm directly on the tape.*

obvious when you divide a length into portions. In the Imperial system, divisions of an inch are read as fractional portions: halves, quarters, eighths, sixteenths and so on. However, since the metric system is decimal, metric fractions are read as some power of ten. Thus ¾ cm is represented as 0.750.

Woodworker's Dueling Rulers: Inches Versus Centimeters

I like the metric system of measurement very much. I can use my calculator to divide any length by any amount and come up with a number that I can read directly on my metric tape measure. I don't have to fool around with converting decimal fractions to thirty-seconds of an inch so that I can read the division lines on my Imperial-scale tape.

When I add lengths together, I don't have to take the time to either convert fractions to powers of ten or go through the mental gymnastics of computing fractions. I do nothing but add the decimal numbers together. The same goes for performing other arithmetical functions.

But do I use the metric system in my woodworking? Not very often. Usually I use metrics only when I'm laying out European hardware whose fastener spacings and offsets are defined within the metric system. Rather than taking the time to convert from metric to Imperial, I simply lay out the hardware positions with my metric tape measure.

There are two fundamental reasons why I don't rely on metrics in my everyday work. The first is that I grew up with the British Imperial System, and I therefore think, and "feel," in feet and inches. I don't know if I could ever picture 60.96

cm as readily as I can picture "a couple of feet." (I can, after all, just look down at my own two feet if I need a reminder.) The second reason is that I try to avoid working with indirect measurements (measurements with numbers) whenever possible, whether they be in Imperial or metric scales. As you will see in the following chapters, once lines are drawn on a set of full-scale plans or layout sticks, most distances can be directly determined, eliminating the need to give a dimension a number. Most of the arithmetical operations, including the division of a distance, can be done directly and graphically on the layout without dealing with any numbers whatsoever.

It is not an issue for me, then, to propose what system of measurement is better for woodworkers here in the U.S. — or anywhere else for that matter. Instead, I find that performing layouts quickly and precisely means avoiding working with direct measurements as soon in the layout stage as possible. Before that point, I suggest you work with whatever measurement system you have the most feeling for; it will likely be the one you will make the fewest errors with.

Chapter 2
Drawing Techniques

M any craftspeople consider the drawing stage in project development to be the most tedious part of woodworking. We are anxious to work with our tools, eager to manipulate fragrant chunks of solid wood into functional and beautiful three-dimensional objects. We often find ourselves exclaiming, "By the time I get these drawings done, I could have built the darn thing!"

It may help for you to know that creating a set of plans for an original piece of furniture need not be a laborious, time-consuming task. With the right techniques and a little practice, the process can not only go smoothly, it can be a whole lot of fun to do. There are, as you will see, plenty of shortcuts available for producing entirely adequate working drawings with a minimum amount of tools and drafting skills.

I'll start by showing you how to create concepts on paper. From there I'll introduce you to the techniques of drafting with mechanical

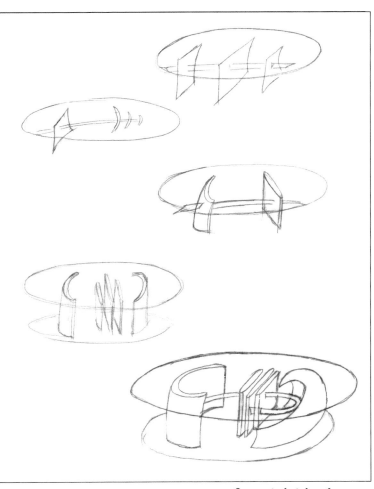

Concept sketches for a coffee table by Jennifer Schwarz.

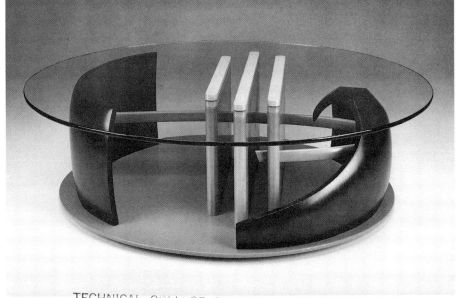

Jennifer Schwarz of Freeland, Washington, arrived at the design of this glass and sculpted walnut coffee table after drawing and refining numerous concept sketches.

Photograph by David L. Browne

aids. The following chapter will get into the nuts and bolts of creating scaled working drawings and full-scale renderings — it is from these life-size drawings that direct measurements can be taken and cutlists developed.

Concept Sketching

This is the fun part. This is conception. This is where you get your first look at the project you're going to build. When you sketch, feel free to draw whatever comes to mind or pencil; don't worry about crisp lines, symmetric angles, fair curves or proper perspectives. Don't worry about proper proportion either; most people tend to draw forms surprisingly close to the ratio of the golden section (see chapter one).

Be prepared to commit a good chunk of time to concept sketching, because it's your best opportunity to work out most of the bugs in the overall look of a piece. Refining the concept now with a series of sketches can save you a lot of time later on. Once you start producing scale drawings, corrections become so time-consuming that you may be tempted to live with a design that doesn't entirely please you.

To create concept sketches, use a soft pencil and easily erasable drawing paper. Avoid sketching on sheets of paper taped to a drawing board. Because the straightest lines and most graceful curves come from a horizontal wrist motion, you want the freedom to move the paper rather than the angle of your hand. Be sure to keep your wrist loose and flexible and, when sketching longer lines, let your arm move with your hand. A useful technique when sketching a complex project is to first block out the major parts of the form with light lines. Keep erasing and redrawing these lines until the overall proportions of the piece look right to you. Then continue to

Developing a concept sketch. Step 1: *Block out the overall form.* **Step 2:** *Commit the form with darker lines and begin to fill in the details.* **Step 3:** *Flesh out the form with the final detailing.*

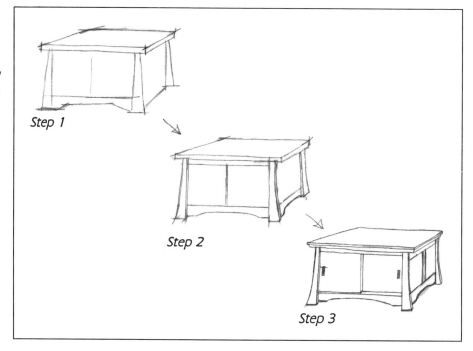

Step 1

Step 2

Step 3

work on the sketch by filling in the details.

When trying to decide among a variety of design options, you may find it helpful to create a "what if" series of sketches. These sketches show the same form enhanced by a variety of different details. Instead of redrawing the basic form over and over again, trace it from the original sketch using a piece of translucent paper, such as vellum. Leave out the areas that will be changed in the "what if" views. Now fill in the new design details and compare it with the original sketch.

Sketching materials and tools

Here's what you'll need to produce concept sketches:

■ **Pencils.** Use a medium hardness (#2 or #2½) pencil with an eraser on the head. (Harder pencils are difficult to erase, and the fine line control they offer isn't necessary when sketching.) Try different brands—I've found there is some variation between pencils of the same hardness number. For me, the Berol #2½ seems just right. Keep a number of sharpened pencils handy, and you won't have to constantly interrupt your flow of ideas to work a point on a pencil.

■ **Paper.** Draw your sketches in a spiral-bound sketchbook with paper specifically formulated for pencil and charcoal drawing; these are available in most art supply stores. Avoid sketching on loose sheets of paper: If you lose a sketch, you will also have lost a record of an idea. And even if that particular idea doesn't make it into this concept's final drawing, it could still have a place in a later project.

Drafting: Producing Drawings With Mechanical Aids

When you have refined your sketches to the point where you're ready to commit dimensions to the concept, it's time to switch over to drafting. At this point you no longer have need for spontaneity. Instead, you must now produce solid information set out in scaled drawings with numbered dimensions. These will be your working drawings.

The process of drafting views of a project to scale allows the craftsperson to see how the actual construction of the piece is going to go. Methods and sequences of joinery become clear, as does the final dimensioning of individual components. The working drawings become a bridge between the freehand concept sketches and the creation of a materials cutlist.

Drafting tools and materials

The size and types of drawings that most woodworkers need to produce for their own use require relatively simple drafting equipment. It is certainly not necessary to have the drafting machines and the selection of layout and inking tools that you would find in the studio of a professional draftsman or architect. I have found the following tools and materials to be more than adequate for my needs.

■ **Drawing board.** Of course it doesn't hurt to have a professional tilt-table drafting board equipped with a mechanical drafting arm. But you can get away with using a parallel bar mounted on a flat piece of 32″ × 48″ plywood. To make the surface smooth, cover the plywood with a sheet of drafting vinyl (available for this purpose through most office supply stores). Unlike the plywood, the vinyl stays smooth even if pricked with a pencil or compass point. A number of commercial portable drawing boards feature a parallel bar with a clip-on plastic drafting head. Portable boards work well for small drawings ($11'' \times 17''$ is pushing it), but restrict you to uncomfortably small scales if you are trying to do a three-view drawing on one piece of paper. I use these boards for single views, sections and detail set-outs.

■ **Rolling ruler.** This device is

A piece of flat plywood covered with a sheet of drafting vinyl and equipped with a parallel rule makes a perfectly adequate drawing board. Note the two types of architect's rules: The triangular-shaped rule contains twelve scales while the flat type rule has eight. A 30°-60° and an adjustable angle template rest against the parallel rule.

This portable plastic drafting board features a built-in parallel rule and a sliding, adjustable angle, drafting head. The table is surprisingly precise and smooth in operation, though its small size limits your choice of scale when doing three-view drawings.

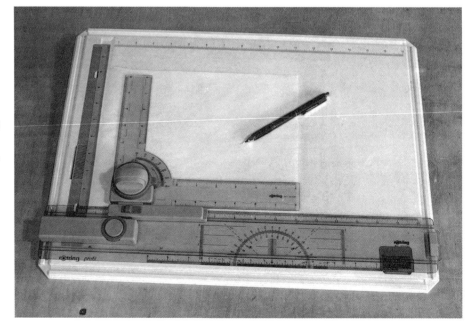

simply a rolling straightedge that maintains parallel lines as you move it along. You still need a scale ruler to mark dimensions. But for smaller drawings (less than 1 square foot), I find that this tool can take the place of a parallel bar and a 90° template. It's accurate and it speeds up the drawing process considerably.

■ **Paper.** The best paper for working drawings is a 16 to 20 pound vellum. This fine-grained, somewhat translucent paper can be purchased in rolls (I use the 42″ size) or single sheets (the sheets are handy for use with a portable board). The good news about vellum is that pencil lines erase easily and thoroughly. In addition, its translucency allows vellum to be used as a tracing paper and as an overlay on a scale grid. Vellum also reproduces well in a blueprint machine. The bad news is that vellum is expensive, even when bought in rolls.

■ **Pencils.** Good, old-fashioned wood pencils are great for concept sketching, but I rarely use them for working drawings. The points dull too quickly, which constantly changes the width of the line. I recommend a set of mechanical pencils with lead sizes ranging from 5mm to 3mm. The leads in these fine mechanical pencils do not need sharpening and maintain constant line widths. The leads do break easily, however, until you develop a light touch. I like to use the HB grade lead because it makes a line dark enough to easily reproduce on a copy machine.

■ **Erasers.** Most mechanical pencils have a small eraser under the top cap. These work well for fine corrections, but you will need additional erasers for bigger goof-ups.

Use the softest eraser that will do the job; on vellum, the classic pink block eraser is perfect. When making fine corrections, use eraser shields to confine the correction to the disaster at hand. Always use a brush to wipe away the debris. If you don't, you will smudge the drawing.

■ **Rulers.** Use an architect's scale ruler for laying out dimensions on the scale drawings. I find the flat ruler with eight scales easier to read and use than the twelve-scale, triangular-shaped rule. To keep the edges crisp and clean, never use the scale ruler for drawing a straight edge. That is what the parallel bar and the angle templates are for.

■ **Angle Templates.** You can get away with an 8″ 45° to 45°, an 8″ 30° to 60°, and a 45° to 90° adjustable. For drawing details, 4″ versions of the 30° to 60° and the 45° to 45° are more pleasant to work with. The templates should be translucent to help you position them on the drawing.

With practice, you can quickly and accurately draw a series of parallel, perpendicular and angled lines with a rolling ruler. Because of the rule's short length, however, it is best suited for drawings of reduced scales or of small dimensions.

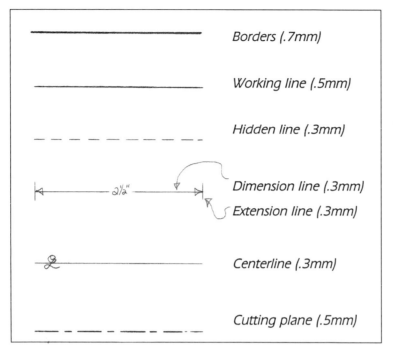

Borders (.7mm)

Working line (.5mm)

Hidden line (.3mm)

2½"   Dimension line (.3mm)

Extension line (.3mm)

Centerline (.3mm)

Cutting plane (.5mm)

Lines used in working drawings.

■ **Protractor.** Use a translucent plastic protractor to mark out angles from a baseline. I like at least a 4″-radius protractor. The larger the radius, the easier the protractor will be to read and the more accurately it will lay out an angle.

■ **Shape Templates.** To speed up drafting, trace circles and ellipses onto your drawing with shape templates. While they might not give you the precise dimension of the shape in the scale of the drawing, the shape will be close enough for most purposes. A set of french curve templates and a set of ship's curves (which are much longer templates, allowing curves of larger radii) let you produce curves of progressively changing radii.

■ **Compass.** A pencil compass is necessary not only to draw circles of varying radii, but, through the magic of graphic geometry, to construct a wide variety of geometric figures. Don't buy a dime store compass for this job—you need more precision than it's capable of giving.

Drawing Lines, Angles and Geometric Figures

A working drawing is nothing more than a bunch of lines that shows you the outlines of a project and what the measurements of it are. But unless the lines performing these different functions are distinctive in some way, the drawing will be difficult, if not impossible, to read. Here are the commonly accepted ways of depicting these lines.

■ **Working lines.** These are the thick lines that show the outside form of the structure. They're also called *visible lines*, because they indicate the visually unobstructed outline of the form.

■ **Hidden lines.** The outside outline of the form hidden from view, and the outlines of internal structures, are drawn in with dashed lines.

■ **Dimension lines.** These lines run alongside the components being measured in the drawing. The lines end in arrows pointing to *extension lines*, which show to what point the measurement is being taken. To avoid confusing an extension line with a working line, never allow the two to touch.

■ **Centerline.** When necessary to show the centerline of the form or a component, use a thin line; indicate its function by placing a *CL* at one end.

■ **Cutting plane.** If a cross section of the structure is to be drawn, the place from which the section is taken is indicated by a *cutting plane* line. Draw it as a solid line broken with dashes.

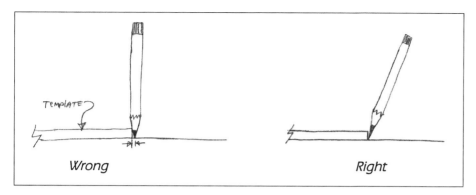

Wrong   Right

Wrong way to draw a line with a drafting template. *Holding the pencil straight up and down creates a gap between the point and the template. As the gap varies, so does the straightness of the line.*

Right way to draw a line with a drafting template. *Angling the pencil so that the point meets the corner between the template and the paper ensures a straight, crisp line.*

Drawing Angles

Once a baseline is established, an angle of any degree can be drawn to it using either angle templates or a protractor and straightedge. There are a couple of techniques you can use to ensure that the angle line begins at the right place and precisely follows the edge of the template or straightedge. (Use these same techniques when laying out cutlines on the wood.)

To begin the angle line precisely on the mark, first place the pencil point on the baseline mark. Then slide the template or straightedge against the pencil. If you try to first align the template to the mark, the parallax between your eye and the thickness of the tool edge will usually throw you off the mark.

When drawing the line itself, hold the pencil at an angle so that the point sits snugly in the corner between the template and the paper. If you hold the pencil shaft straight up and down, chances are you will produce a wavering line.

Bisecting an angle

The simplest way to bisect an angle is to set the protractor angle to half the original full angle and then draw in the line with a straightedge. If, however, the angle is not a whole number and is thus hard to read, or if you want absolute precision, use a compass to find the bisect angle geometrically. Note that the larger the radius of the arc in step one, the more accurately you can place the bisecting line.

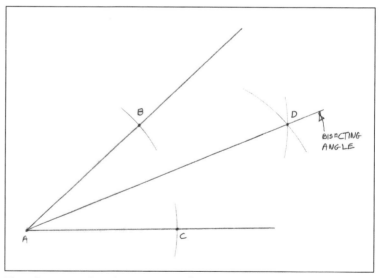

Bisecting an angle using geometry. **Step 1:** *Set a compass point at* **A** *and swing an arc through the two angle lines, creating intersections* **B** *and* **C**. **Step 2:** *Set the compass point on point* **B** *and swing an arc in the area between the lines. Repeat at point* **C**, *creating an intersection at point* **D**. **Step 3:** *Connect a line from point* **A** *to point* **D** — *this is the bisecting angle.*

Drawing Circles and Arcs

Circles are most easily drawn by tracing them through a circle template. You will, however, have to draw a horizontal and vertical axis through the intended center of the circle to position the template.

If the template doesn't have a circle of the correct size, place a compass against a scale ruler and set the desired radius—make sure you're using the correct scale. Swing the circle around the center point indicated on the plans. To ensure that the circle comes out at the precise radius, most draftspeople sharpen the compass's pencil to a chiseled edge, not a point; orient the chiseled edge toward the outside of the circle.

Sometimes it's necessary to draw a portion of a circle tangent to two straight lines to indicate a rounded corner. Note that the technique used when the lines are perpendicular to each other is different than when the lines come together at an angle.

Occasionally you may need to draw an arc along a straight line (to show, for instance, the shape of an arched table apron). If you know the height you wish the arc to be, and you know where it begins and ends, you can find the radius of the arc by using the formula shown in the illustration.

In chapter five, which covers laying out cutlines on the material, I will introduce you to other techniques and tools for laying out circles, ellipses, arc tangents and arches that are more appropriate for full-scale applications.

Drawing a round corner at the intersection of two perpendicular lines. Step 1: *Set a compass to the desired radius of the corner and swing an arc through the intersecting lines, creating points* B *and* C. *Step 2: From point* B, *and then from point* C, *swing arcs to create an intersection at point* D. *Step 3: Without changing the setting of the compass, place the point at* D *and swing an arc connecting points* B *and* C.

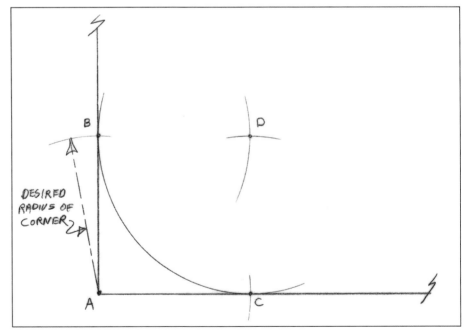

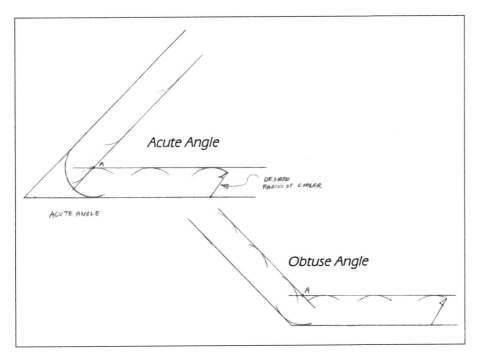

Acute Angle

ACUTE ANGLE

DESIRED
RADIUS OF CORNER

Obtuse Angle

Drawing rounded corners at the intersection of angles other than 90°. *The steps for both acute and obtuse angles are the same:* Step 1: *Set the compass to the desired radius of the rounded corner and swing a series of arcs to the inside of the angle.* Step 2: *Draw straight lines across the tops of the arcs, creating an intersection point at A.* Step 3: *Without changing the setting of the compass, fix the point at A and swing an arc connecting the intersecting lines — creating your rounded corner.*

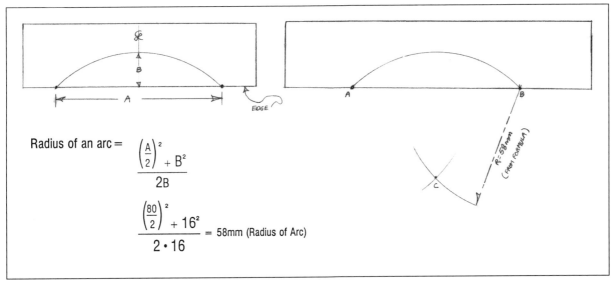

EDGE

Radius of an arc $= \dfrac{\left(\dfrac{A}{2}\right)^2 + B^2}{2B}$

$\dfrac{\left(\dfrac{80}{2}\right)^2 + 16^2}{2 \cdot 16} = 58mm$ (Radius of Arc)

Drawing an arc along a straightedge. Step 1: *Determine the radius of the arc from the formula and fix the compass at this distance.* Step 2: *Swing arcs below the line using center points A and B, creating intersection C.* Step 3: *Set the point of the compass at C and swing an arc through points A and B.*

Formula to determine a radius when given the height and width of an arc relative to an edge. *Where A = the width along the edge, B = the height from the edge. Here, width A = 80mm and height B = 16mm. Use the formula for the radius of an arc given in the illustration above.*

Construction of a pentagon. Step 1: *Draw a baseline at the desired location of one facet of the pentagon. Fix points A and B at the width of the facet.* **Step 2:** *Use the formula to derive the construction angle and erect lines from A and B to create an intersection at C.* **Step 3:** *Set a compass to the distance C-A and swing a circle through B and back to A.* **Step 4:** *Reset the compass to distance A-B and step this distance off around the circle, from A. Connecting these points yields a pentagon.*

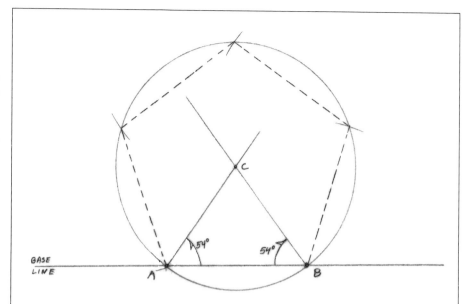

Distance AB = Desired width of polygon's facet

Polygon construction angle formula:

$$90° - \frac{180}{5} = 54°$$

5 (pentagon) = Number of sides

Drawing Polygons

Many polygons turn up in woodworking projects, more than you might guess at first thought. For example, the tops of small tables are not always squares or rectangles, but are often six- or eight-sided polygons. Table legs and the "pencil posts" of bedsteads are often designed with more than four sides. So take a moment to learn how to draw polygons of a varying number of sides. Stretching your drafting skills can only help increase your ability and desire to explore other design options.

A polygon is defined by the number of sides it contains. Thus, a five-sided polygon is a *pentagon*, while an eight-sided one is an *octagon*. To construct a polygon of any number of sides, you need only know what angle the sides make to one another. To find the construction angle, which is half this angle, use the following formula:

construction angle = 90 - 180/N

(where N is the number of sides)

Techniques for Drawing Irregular Curves

When creating an original piece of furniture, there is often the need to design, and thus to draw, curved surfaces that are not fixed by the radius of a circle. Sweeps of chair legs, headboards of beds, and the arches of support brackets are a few examples of curves that are designed with constantly changing radii.

To draw an irregular curve on a working drawing, begin by lightly sketching in the curve in its approximate position. Refer to your concept sketches to help you retain the same "feeling" in the curve. When it looks about right, compare the curve to your selection of french and ship's curve templates. Chances are good that you will find the sketched curve comes very close to a curve offered by one or more of the templates.

Notice that I said "or more." It's often the case that one end of the curve will match one template's curve while the opposite end matches another. But if you can't find a template that matches the sketch line to your satisfaction, use a leaded curve bar or a plastic slip curve to mimic the sketch line. I tend to use these flexible curves as a last resort because they rarely make a very fair line (one that smoothly changes in radius). When you're happy with the match, darken in the line.

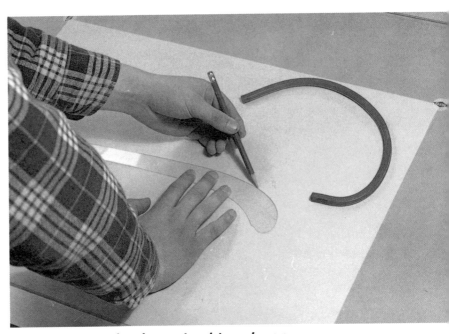

Drawing a line to a french curve template produces a smooth curve of constantly changing radius. The plastic-coated lead bar sitting in view on the table is adjustable to any type of curve, though the line it produces is not always as smooth as that of a template.

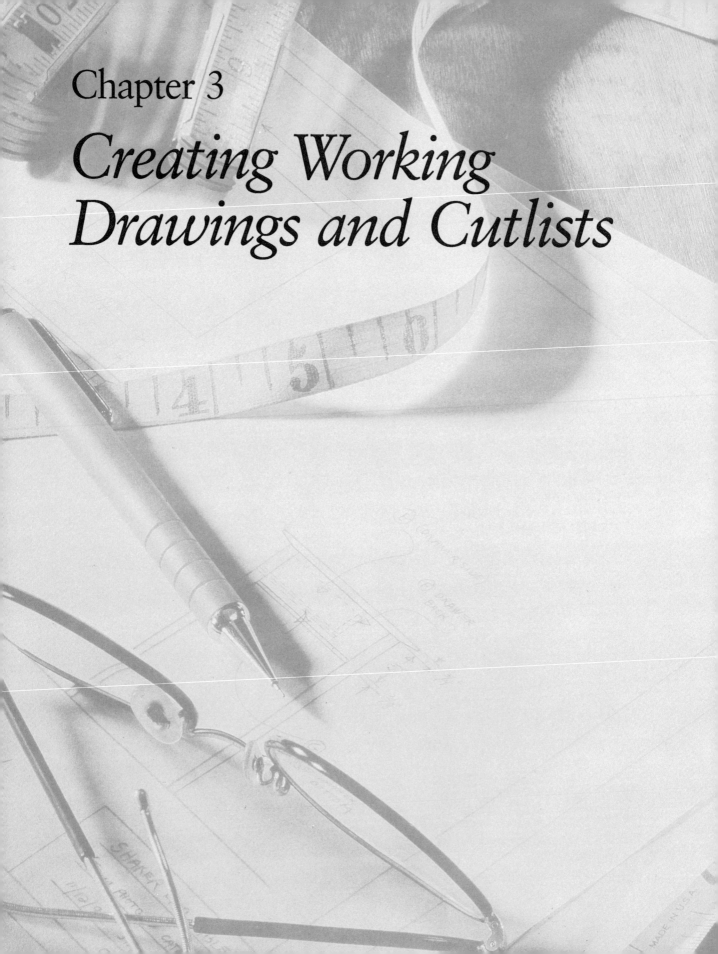

Chapter 3
Creating Working Drawings and Cutlists

Once you conceive a project with a series of concept sketches (or find a photograph or drawing of a piece you would like to build), the next step is to create a set of working drawings. Because these drawings define your concept with scaled dimensions, they show you how the various views and details of the piece relate to one another in true proportion. This gives you a chance to fuss about and adjust things on paper before you start cutting into the wood (a less-erasable proposition). When everything looks right, you'll use these drawings to create cutlists for the components of the project.

The first working drawing that I produce for a project is a three-view *orthographic projection*. This drawing, rendered at a reduced scale (usually ¼ of full size), shows face-on views of the front, side and top of the piece as individual views (also called *elevations*). Note that each component is given a dimension and a part symbol.

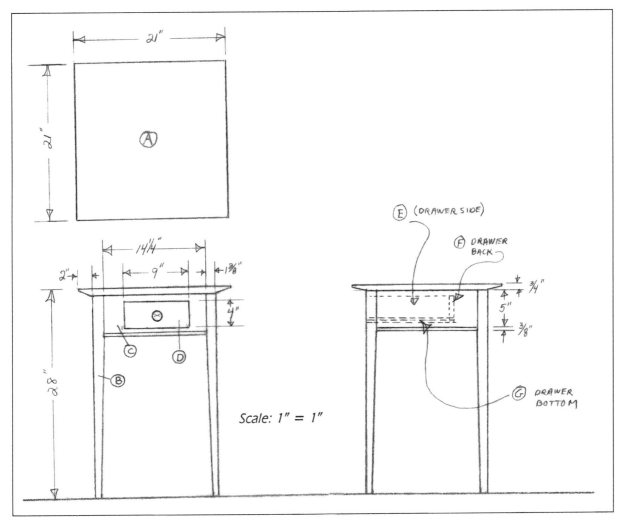

Scale: 1" = 1"

Three-view orthographic projection.

Shaker end table (derived from photo in catalog), 11/12/92. Copyright 1992 Jim Tolpin.

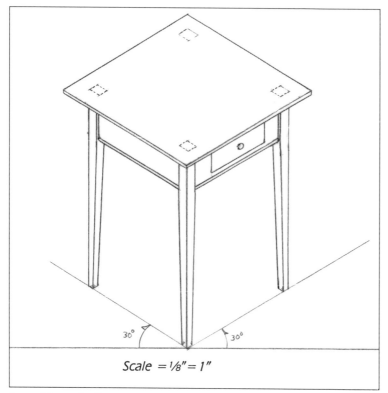

Isometric projection.

Scale = 1/8" = 1"

30°   30°

To see what these views look like in their actual relationship to one another, I next draw an *isometric projection*. This working drawing provides an aerial quarter-view of the elevations assembled together. Unlike a perspective drawing, this type of projection does not distort or foreshorten any of the views. And because all the lines are drawn parallel and to their true scaled dimensions, it is much easier to draw than a perspective.

Except when designing the simplest of projects, I go on from these reduced-dimensioned drawings to produce a full-scale, three-view rendering. Seeing the piece at its actual size, I can now, with greater confidence, tell if anything is still amiss with the design. In the past, all too often I have found that proportions and details that looked great in a reduced scale simply didn't work when built to their true dimensions. Sometimes I'll even take the full-scale drawing to the proposed site of the piece to see if its overall dimensions will work harmoniously with the scale of its surroundings.

Another very important reason

Drawing out a design to full-scale on a large sheet of paper ensures that all the dimensions and proportions of a piece are correct. On this drawing of a Shaker end table, I have attached a piece of wood to the drawing to represent the overhang of the top. Setting the full-scale rendering upright and at floor level creates a surprisingly accurate representation of the piece.

why I render a project in full-scale is that it gives me a way to obtain direct measurements for dimensioning components, molding profiles and joinery. This virtually eliminates the kinds of errors that may creep into a project when I work only from dimension numbers on a reduced-scale drawing. (Details of making story poles and cutlists from full-scale drawings are covered later in this chapter and chapter four.)

Producing a Three-View Drawing From a Concept Sketch

Don't start drafting until you have a clear mind and a clear table. You're going to need plenty of room in both places. Try to schedule your time so you'll be uninterrupted—except for the most simple projects, you'll need at least half a day.

Begin by taping a large sheet of vellum (42″ wide by 32″ high is usually adequate) to the drafting surface. Draw a border around the edge with a wide pencil (0.7mm) and create a legend box in the lower right-hand corner. In this box place the following information:

■ Your name and the client's name.

■ The date of the original drawing. Leave room for a new date if the drawing is revised.

■ The name of the piece, if any. If a reproduction, say where and when the original piece was built and by whom.

■ If this will be a limited-edition piece, say so specifically: "Only X number of pieces to be built from this drawing."

■ A copyright symbol followed by the year and your last name.

■ After building the piece, you may want to note in this legend what wood(s) the piece was made from, how much the materials cost, and how many hours of labor were consumed. This information will prove invaluable for future reference if the same, or a similar, project is to be built.

Choose the concept sketch (or combination of sketches) whose form and details you wish to commit to the three-view drawing, and tape them to the top of the drawing board. Then draw a horizontal baseline about a quarter to a third of the way from the bottom of the paper.

Choosing a scale

Quarter-scale ($\frac{1}{4}″ = 1″$) works well for most furniture projects. It lets you fit all three views onto one sheet of paper while allowing adequate space to clearly define details. For unusually large projects you may need to downsize to $\frac{1}{8}$ scale; in this case, draw complex details to a larger, more readable scale in a separate drawing.

Take a close look at the quarter-scale on your architect's rule. While you can use this scale to make this reduction, note that this scale is really set up for $\frac{1}{4}″ = 1′$: The first "foot" is divided into twelve parts for marking off inches. Because you want to be able to measure portions of an inch in the scale of $\frac{1}{4}″ = 1″$, instead use the three scale. Here you'll find a $\frac{1}{4}″$-long unit broken into eight divisions. Use these divisions to represent eighths of an inch. (If you want to go to an eighth reduction, use the $1\frac{1}{2}$ scale where there are four divisions over $\frac{1}{8}″$. You can use each division to represent $\frac{1}{4}″$).

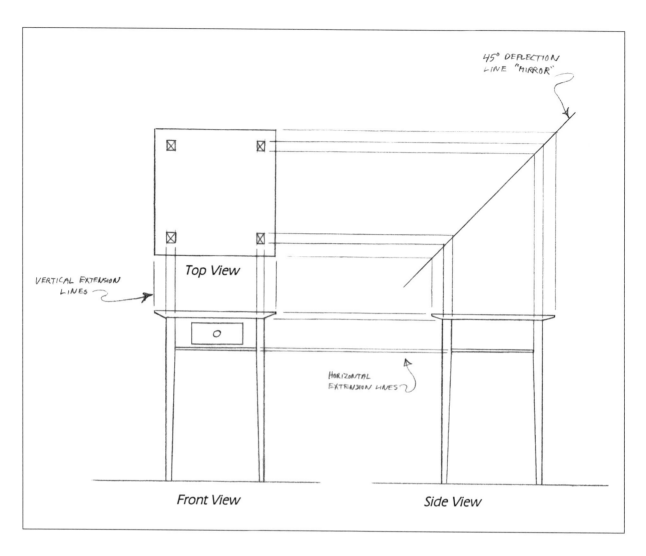

Top View

45° DEFLECTION
LINE "MIRROR"

VERTICAL EXTENSION
LINES

HORIZONTAL
EXTENSION LINES

Front View

Side View

Setting out a three-view orthographic drawing.

Establishing the front, top and side views

Toward the left-hand side of the paper, block out the front view of the piece on the baseline with a light pencil line. To size the width and height of the basic form, refer to dimensions derived from a photograph or catalog drawing (page 32), or use the dimensions you have designed. Lightly fill in the front view with the other elements of the piece, such as a face frame and door and drawer faces.

Your eye will tell you if the proportions of the scaled drawing ap-proximate those of the concept sketch. When you've finished block-ing in the front view, you may wish to check the proportions of the piece against those prescribed by the golden section (unless you are spe-cifically designing the piece to an-other proportioning system). When you're satisfied with the overall ap-pearance of the view, draw *working lines* (page 20) over the light block-ing lines to finalize the outline of the piece and its elements. Now you're ready to create the top view.

Establish the overall width of the top view by extending vertical lines (90° to the baseline) up from either end of the front view. You can also establish the widths of other elements in the top view by extending additional lines from the front view.

To determine the depth of the piece in the top view, refer to your concept sketch or to your predetermined dimensions. Lay the depth out to scale along a vertical line, then draw the horizontal lines defining the front and back of the top view. Draw in the other elements of the top view to scale, and double-check the proportions.

Unless the sides of the piece are asymmetrical, you need only draw one side view. As a right-hander, I tend to draw from left to right, so I like to place this view to the right of the front view.

With the front and top views drawn in, the height and width of the side view is already established. Extend the dimensions from these two drawings over to the location of the side view. Begin by extending a horizontal line from the front view to indicate the overall height of the piece. Also extend horizontal lines from the elements in the front view

that relate to those that will appear in the side view.

To use the top view to determine the width of the side view, build a mirror: a line tilted at 45° and set to the right of the top view and over the intended location of the side view. As you bring each line over horizontally from the top view, it intersects the 45° angle line and is reflected at a 90° angle down to the baseline. These lines define the width of the side view.

If the side of the structure is not 90° to the front face, the projection method I just outlined will not produce a true-to-scale side view but one that is foreshortened. In this case, produce the side view as follows: First, project horizontal lines over from the front view to establish the height of the elements of the side view. Instead of reflecting down extension lines, determine the widths of the side view by scaling the dimensions directly from the top view with an architect's rule. Mark these measurements along the appropriate horizontal extension lines and then draw in the vertical outlines of the side view.

Producing a side-view of an angled side. Problem: *You cannot use a mirror line to project the side of the top view to the baseline—distance B is less than distance A, so the side view would be foreshortened.* **Solution:** *Use a scale or set a compass to measure distance A. Transfer the distance directly to the horizontal line extended over from the front view. Drop lines to the baseline from the distance marks.*

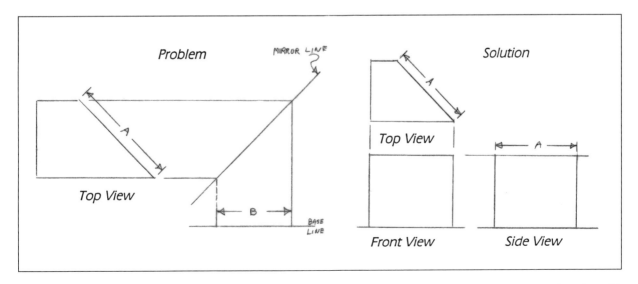

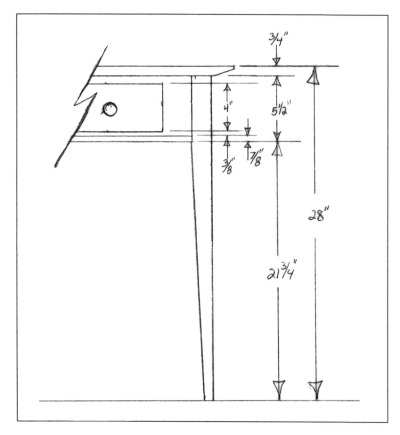

Setting in dimension lines. The overall dimension (here, total height) is drawn to the outside of all other dimensions. In general, the smallest dimensions are kept closest to the object.

one horizontal and one vertical. To keep the views uncluttered, I set out interior details of joints away from a view, sometimes at a larger scale. I also don't label the components of the piece with part numbers or letters unless I know there won't be a full-scale drawing.

It is absolutely essential, however, that you completely describe the three views with dimensions. Give each component a dimension line, being careful to correctly place the extension lines (see chapter two). Work your way out from the smallest elements of the components, to the components themselves, to the final dimension line indicating the overall size of the structure. Be thorough so you don't have to constantly dig out a scale ruler when using the working drawing to develop a cutlist or when transferring measurements to a full-scale drawing.

Finishing Up the Three-View Drawing

After outlining the three views, fill in any details shown in the concept sketches. If there are irregular curves to be drawn to scale, do this using the methods outlined in the last chapter. If a detail is going to be repeated a number of times, you can either draw it once and roughly sketch in the others, or you can make a separate master drawing and trace the shape through the vellum at each location.

I generally don't bother to draw in underlying structures and joint details in three-view drawings if I intend to produce a full-scale rendering of the project. But if I do want to show the internal structures in the three-view drawing, I'll do so by drawing two sections of the piece,

Developing a Three-View Drawing From a Photograph

It is entirely possible to develop working drawings from nothing more than a single photograph (or even a sketch in a catalog). It helps greatly, of course, if the photograph was taken from a point slightly above and to one side of the piece. The resulting image then gives you an aerial view of all three sides of the piece, similar to the viewpoint of an isometric projection.

You must, however, somehow predetermine the overall height, width and depth of the piece before beginning the drawing process. If the photograph or sketch is from a catalog or design book, the dimensions are often given in a caption.

Otherwise, you'll have to make an educated guess based on standard dimensions for the particular type of furniture. If you're lucky, the photograph itself reveals clues to the piece's overall size. For example, I derived the dimensions for a Stickley bookcase from a picture in a catalog by using the height of the encyclopedias posed on the shelves as a scale reference. I found a scale on the architect's rule that measured the books at about 9″ (which I assumed standard for these books), and then I used this scale to find the overall width and height of the bookcase. I guessed the depth of the case based on my knowledge of the depth of the books on the shelves.

To dimension a piece from a photograph, use double-sided tape to hold the picture to the center of a piece of vellum fixed to a drawing board. Then hold a straightedge parallel to the outlines of the face view of the piece in the photograph and extend the outside height and width lines onto the vellum.

To dimension the heights of elements such as drawer faces and doors, lay an architect's rule across the extended overall height line and baseline. Now that you know the height of the piece, find a scale that shows the height between these two lines. You'll probably have to tilt the ruler to get it to read this number on one of the scales. Now draw a line at the angle the ruler makes with the extension lines. Extend the height lines of the doors and drawer face until they intersect the ruled line. Read the height of these elements directly by measuring between the intersection points along the ruled line with the ruler. Be sure to use the same scale that you used

to read the overall height of the piece.

To find the width of the elements, extend lines up vertically from the drawing. Now follow the same procedure with the scale ruler as described above. Once all the elements have been dimensioned, you can lay out the elevations of the three views to the scale of your choice.

With a photograph of a piece of furniture taped to a piece of vellum, I use a scale rule laid across horizontal extension lines to read off the height of the door and the drawer faces. Angling the ruler aligns the overall height dimension on the ruled scale with the base and top extension lines.

build a scale model or a mock-up from the three-view drawings that I've generated.

To save the labor and money a full-scale mock-up might require, I see if I can get a good feeling from a scale model first. Unless the piece features compound curves, I use architect's foamcore modeling board to represent the three views of the project. This material is fun to work with. It shows dimension marks clearly and it cuts cleanly with a craft knife. I assemble the components with pins and white glue. To deal with compound curves, I shape modeling clay (Plasticine) or carve soft wood (balsa or basswood) to the desired form.

To keep things simple, I lay out the parts of the scale model to the same scale I used in the three-view drawing. Avoiding scale changes reduces the chances of making an error when transferring the dimensions over to the model stock. This also makes it easy to transfer any changes I make to the models back to the working drawing.

The miracle material for creating full-size mock-ups is corrugated cardboard. It's readily available in the form of discarded boxes (appliance stores and lumberyards are a good bet for larger pieces) or as $4' \times 8'$ sheets from your local paper supply house (ask your stationery store). Mock-ups for case-like projects such as bureaus and wall cabinets usually require only a single thickness of cardboard sheeting to represent the views. Join the sheets together at the corners with some packing tape.

Thicker components of a project can be portrayed in cardboard by folding or stacking sheets to the ap-

(Above) *Foam core modeling board is an excellent material for making reduced-scale prototypes of case-type furniture. These models are made to the same scale as their three-view isometric projections ($\frac{1}{4}$" = 1").*

(Right) *Building a full-scale prototype of a piece of furniture ensures that the proportions and style of a project are visually pleasing from any viewing angle. I built this model of a Shaker end table quickly and without cost from taped together sheets of $\frac{1}{8}$" thick corrugated cardboard.*

Making Models and Mock-Ups

There are certain projects (chairs are notorious for this) that are so problematic in design that no amount of concept sketches or working drawings (even at full scale) gives you a feeling for what the piece will really look like when its all put together. Unless you have access to a computer drawing system, there's just no way to make a drawing that shows the piece from every angle. My solution is to forge ahead and

propriate thickness. White glue or hot, melted glue from a glue gun works well for laminating. Shape the laminated layers to the form you wish with saws and rasps or Surforms.

Transfer the dimensions of a mock-up back to a working drawing by recording the full-scale dimensions onto a rough sketch. Then read these dimensions on the appropriate scale of the architect's rule as you draw in the elevations in the three-view drawing.

To dimension curved components onto the working drawing, disassemble the mock-up and lay the curve on a grid sized to the scale of the drawing. For example, if the drawing has been done in quarter-scale, make the grid in 1″ squares. The intersection of the curved lines on this grid then readily transfer to a ¼″ grid on the scale drawing. (Details of this procedure will be covered on page 36.)

Creating an Isometric Drawing From a Three-View Drawing

Create an isometric projection from a three-view drawing by first establishing a baseline and then erecting two 30° angles away from a central point. These lines now become the baselines for the front and side elevations. Lightly draw in the "footprint" of the piece by laying out the overall length of the front elevation and the overall width of the side elevation on the angled baselines. Extend these dimensions into the isometric view parallel to the baselines as shown in the drawing. Again, be sure to use light lines—most of them will be hidden by the front and side elevations.

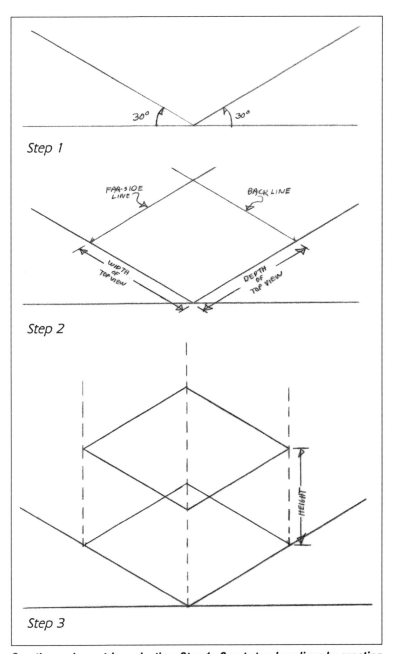

Creating an isometric projection. Step 1: *Create two baselines by erecting 30° angled lines up from a point established along a horizontal line.* Step 2: *Draw in the "footprint" of the top view along the baselines. Extend the view "into" the isometric projection by drawing the lines of the back and the far side. Keep these lines parallel to the baselines.* Step 3: *Establish the actual top view by first extending vertical lines up from the corners of the footprint. Measure up along one line to the overall height of the front view. Draw in the outline of the top view parallel to the baselines.*

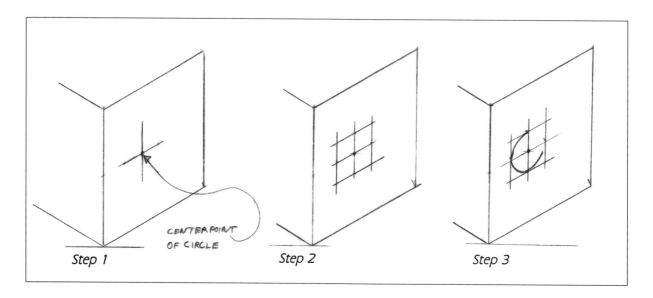

CENTER POINT OF CIRCLE

Step 1   Step 2   Step 3

Sketching a circle on an isometric projection. Step 1: *Establish the center point of the circle (by measuring from an orthographic drawing) and draw in vertical and horizontal (30°) axis lines.* **Step 2:** *Measure the diameter of the circle along the axis and draw a square around the center point.* **Step 3:** *Sketch in an arc in each quadrant of the square. The result is an ellipse.*

Now "raise" the structure by extending vertical lines (90° to the original baseline) from the corners of the footprint up to the height of the top view as scaled from the three-view drawing. Draw in the top with parallel lines. The resulting form is an isometric cube drawn to the maximum dimensions of the structure. All the other lines of the piece will occur within this cube.

Now fill in the details of the elevations by taking scaled measurements from the three-view drawing and transferring them directly to the isometric grid. You may find it helpful to place isometric grid paper under the vellum as an aid to sketching in these details with a straightedge. Without the grid, use a 90° and a 30° template to draw in the lines. Erase the construction lines used to raise the top view as they become obstructed by the elevations.

One tricky part to detailing an isometric projection is the rendering of circles. Because of the angled baseline, a circle appears as an ellipse in the isometric plane of the views. You can sketch in an ellipse

by the following technique: First, draw a vertical and a horizontal (30°) axis through the desired center point location of the circle. Now measure the diameter of the circle along both axes and erect a square around the center point. (This is a little tricky also: A square is actually a parallelogram in the isometric plane.) Finally, lightly sketch in an arc in each quadrant of the square. When it looks good, darken in the line to blend the arcs together into an ellipse.

Developing Full-Scale Drawings From Three-View Drawings or Mock-Ups

It would be nice if you could take a scaled three-view working drawing and run it through a copy machine to blow it up to full size. Actually, I've tried this, only to discover that the drawing was just not accurate enough. Most machines in use today distort the images up to 1/4" when blowing up a quarter-scale drawing to full size. Until they come up with a distortion-free copy machine, this is how I make a full-scale working drawing:

Start by taping butcher's paper or rolled tracing paper to a smooth piece of plywood larger than the size of the project. Then, using a long straightedge, lightly pencil in a baseline as close to the bottom of the paper as possible (assuming the baseline represents the floor). The drawing, when set upright, will appear at about the same height as intended for the actual piece. Now place a centerline where you wish to center the front view. Draw the centerline perfectly square to the baseline. Use a set of trammel points to act as a large compass (see chapter four) to construct a perpendicular.

To transfer a dimension from the scaled drawing to full scale, read the measurement given along the dimension line and lay this out on the paper at that dimension ($1'' = 1''$). Lay out the full-scale's three views by following the same basic procedure described earlier in this chapter for laying out reduced-scale working drawings. Use the baseline and centerline as reference points for measuring off parallel height and width lines.

If the project includes an irregular curve, overlay the curve on the drawing with a grid of ¼" squares. Also create a 1" square grid on the full-scale drawing in the area where this curve is to appear. Use the architect's scale rule to read the intersections of the curve on the ¼" grid lines (remember that the three scale provides you with ⅛" increments at this scale). Transfer these intersection points at full scale to the 1" grid on the full-scale drawing. Then connect the intersection points with an adjustable curve tool or a batten stick (as described in chapter five).

You can reverse this technique to transfer the lines of a curved component on a mock-up to a scaled working drawing. Disassemble the mock-up if necessary and lay the curved component on a 1" grid. Trace the curve onto the grid. Now measure the intersection points and transfer the points at ¼ scale to a ¼" grid on the working drawing. Connect the points with french curves or an adjustable curve.

Grid technique for transferring curves to another scale. Step 1: *Overlap a ¼" grid over the area containing the curve.* Step 2: *Measure intersections of the curve on the ¼" grid with a scale rule (use three-scale on an architect's rule). Transfer these points at full-scale to a 1" grid.* Step 3: *Connect the intersection points with a french curve or an adjustable curve.*

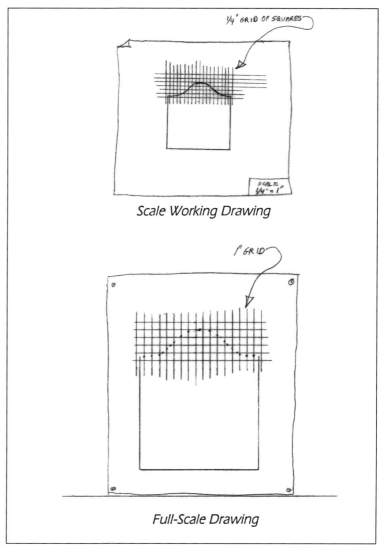

Scale Working Drawing

Full-Scale Drawing

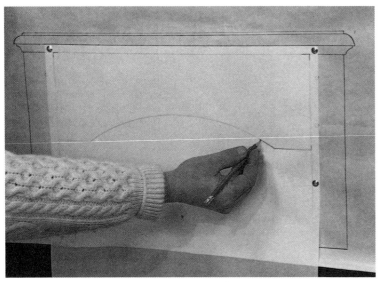

This full-scale rendering of a piece of furniture gives me the ability to quickly develop full-size templates of complex shapes. Here, I am tracing the shape of an arched apron through a piece of vellum taped to the drawing.

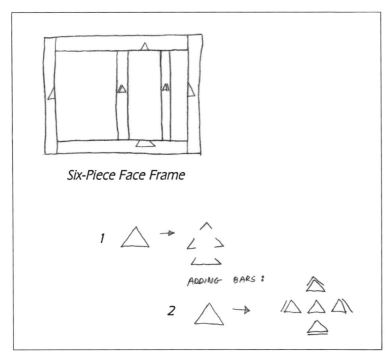

Six-Piece Face Frame

ADDING BARS :

Cabinetmaker's "pyramid" orientation marking system. Step 1: *To orient the outside components of an assembly to each other, mark the outside face with a portion of a pyramid.* **Step 2:** *Inside components may be marked by adding bars.*

To show underlying structures on full-scale drawings, I usually draw them in with a pencil of a different color. This is much faster, and less confusing visually, than covering the drawing with dashed lines.

Making Full-Scale Templates

Many projects have components that must be cut to complex shapes, such as irregularly curved chair back supports or stepped table aprons. The best way I have found to transfer these shapes onto the wood is with a full-size template made from ⅛" plywood *doorskin*. If you have brought the shape up from the reduced drawings to full scale with the grid system I described, you are already halfway toward creating a template.

The next step is to trace the shape of the component drawn on the full-scale rendering onto a sheet of tracing vellum. Tape the paper over the area to be traced, then use a soft pencil to copy the underlying shape. Remove the vellum and tack it in place on the template stock (already cut to width and length) with a piece of carbon paper placed in between. Retrace the shape through the carbon paper.

An alternative to vellum is heavyweight (at least 0.006" thick) Mylar. Tack the Mylar over the full-scale rendering and mark the outline with a pen made to write on plastic (check your local photography store for a photographic marker pen). Remove the tracing and cut it to the lines with scissors or a utility knife. The cut out Mylar shape becomes the template. Tape it in place on the wood and trace around it with a sharp pencil.

Developing Cutlists From Working Drawings

The first step in developing cutlists that tell you exactly how and where each piece of wood is to be cut is to generate a bill of materials from the working drawings. Get this information by reading the dimensions written on the scaled three-view drawing or by measuring directly from a full-scale rendering.

The bill of materials is a good way to list the parts. Note that each part is represented by a symbol, usually an encircled letter. To help orient the parts correctly during assembly, you can add an orientation symbol as well, using the very effective "pyramid" marking system commonly used by cabinetmakers. After recording each part in the bill of materials, double-circle the part symbol in the drawing to show that it has been recorded.

Enter the widths and lengths in the bill of materials to the full dimensions of the pieces. In this way, you'll allow sufficient material for tenons, tongues and overlaps. Unless you note otherwise, let the length run with the grain of the wood.

From Bill of Materials to Master Cutlists

Once the bill of materials has been completed, double-check the working drawing to be sure all the symbols have been double-circled. Then compile the information onto master cutlists. Depending on the complexity of the project, you may need one for solid stock and another for plywood components. The example in the drawing illustrates the way I would make up the master cutlist for the Shaker table project cited in

BILL OF MATERIALS   Page 1

Job: _Shaker end table_

Symbol	Part	Quan.	Dimensions		Stock	
			Width	Length	Solid	Ply
A	Top	1	21″	21″	¾″ C	
B	Legs	4	1⅜″	27¼″	1⅜″M	
C	Aprons	4	5⅜″	15″	¾″ M	
D	Drawer Face	1	4″	9″	¾″ P	
E	Drawer Slide	2	3⅛″	16″	½″ P	
F	Drawer Back	1	3⅛″	8⅛″	½″ P	
G	Drawer Bottom	1	7⅝″	15½″		¼″M

C = Cherry   M = Hard Maple   P = Pine

Bill of materials (for the Shaker table in the drawing on page 27).

MASTER CUTLIST — Page 1

Job: *Shaker end table*

B *Legs (1⅜″ Maple)* *1⅜″* *27¼″ 4*	*A* *Top (¾″ Cherry)* *21″* *21″ 1*
C *Aprons (¾″ Maple)* *5⅜″* *15″ 4*	*D* *Drawer Face (¾″ Maple)* *4″* *9″ 1*
E Drawer Sides (½″ Pine) *F 3⅛″* *16″ 2* *8⅛″ 1*	*G Drawer Bottom* *(¼″ Maple Ply)* *7⅝″* *15½″ 1*

Master cutlist (derived from the Shaker table's bill of materials).

the bill of materials sample.

In general, collate the components by parts function, listing the length of the parts under each width. Start with the widest and thickest stock, working your way down to the smallest pieces. This works in your favor later on when laying out the boards, as you generally want to account for the largest pieces first. The waste areas are then used for smaller components. Also notice that any components that are not perfectly square-sided are given a graphic to remind you what is going to have to be done to the piece. Make sure that you double-circle the part symbol on the bill of material table as each piece is recorded on the cutlist.

To the right of the lengths listed under each thickness and width column are "scratch" marks that indicate the number of pieces needed of this size. Avoid using numerals, since this could confuse you. As you lay out each piece in the graphic picture boards, account for it by making a scratch mark to the left of the length number. When the scratch marks are equal on either side, you'll know that all the components of this size have been laid out. At that time, draw a line through the length measurement.

From Master Cutlists to Picture Boards

After you've completed the master cutlists, lay the sizes of the components out on graphic pictures of the solid stock or sheets of plywood from which the pieces will be cut. Be sure to account for the kerfs (widths of the cuts), and for defects that must be cut around in the solid stock (more on this in chapter five).

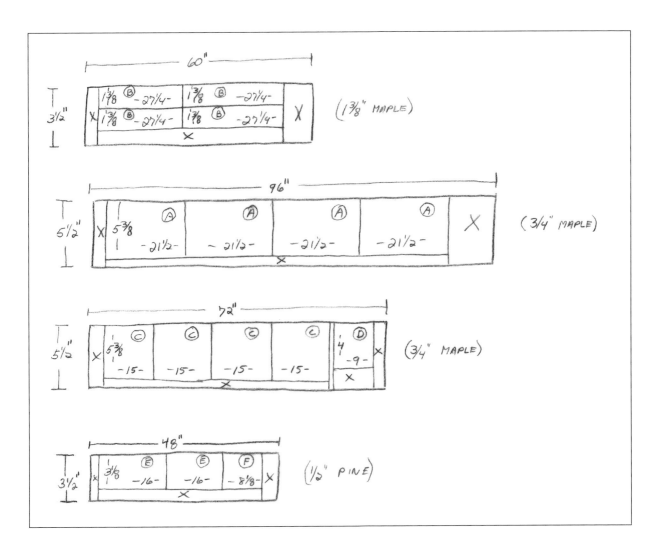

If you devote some time and a good bit of head scratching to this process, you'll minimize the amount of waste material.

In the next two chapters, we'll finally move from all this paper-working to real woodworking. I'll begin by introducing you to the lay-out tools for measuring and making the marks on the wood. Then I'll show you some good techniques for getting the information from these drawings down onto the actual wood itself.

Picture-board layout for the Shaker table.

Chapter 4
Measurement and Layout Tools

O nce you've described your project with working drawings and cutting diagrams, you're ready to lay out the cuts on the wood. This requires a new set of skills and, happily for tool lovers, a new set of marking, measuring and layout tools. But while many of the tools are readily available at the local hardware store, some can't even be found through the specialty mail-order tool suppliers listed in the back of this book. You'll have to make them. Lest the thought of this prove overwhelming, be aware that some of the most useful layout tools are simply pieces of wood with lines drawn on them.

The Work Surface

Before tackling these hand tools, make sure you have an adequate workbench upon which to mark, cut and test-fit the components. Give yourself at least a 3' square of flat, level and stable work surface set to a comfortable height (34″ to 38″ above the floor). You can test your workbench for flatness with a pair of shop-made winding sticks. Depending on the construction of your bench, you can either shim the legs or plane the solid woodwork surface until the winding sticks sight parallel from one end of the bench to the other.

Marking Tools

The ubiquitous carpenter's pencil — the pencil that has the shape of a flattened octagon and contains a rectangular, rather than round, lead core — is far more useful to a woodworker than a normal #2 pencil for

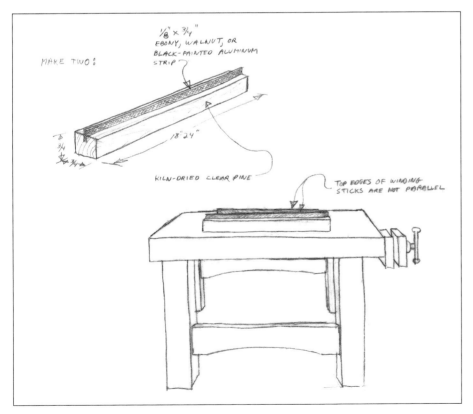

Checking a surface for twist with winding sticks. *Set a pair of winding sticks on the bench, one at either end. If the surface is free of twist, the top edges of the sticks will appear parallel.*

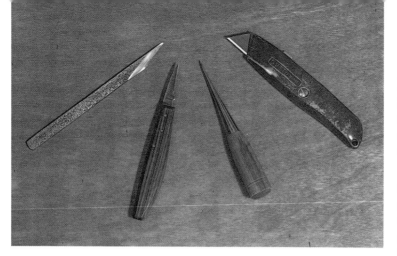

Because knives mark the wood with crisp, narrow lines, I use them instead of a pencil to lay out cutlines with precision. When marking a line parallel with the grain of the wood, a scratch awl (shown between the knives) often makes a more visible line than does a knife.

a number of reasons. Its somewhat harder lead allows the point to stay sharp much longer when used on coarse wood surfaces, and the lead's rectangular shape is quick and easy to sharpen with a utility knife, a common woodworker's tool.

A carpenter's pencil is not, however, the best marking tool for every situation. On very dark woods, such as walnut for example, use a white artist's pencil (the Berol Verithin #734 works well). On rough lumber, mark the layout lines and identification symbols with either chalk or a colored timber crayon. To lay out long, straight lines, you can modify a standard builder's chalk line reel to make a clean, fine line. All you need do is substitute a thinner gauge cotton line for the standard cord (check a local fabric store for crochet cotton).

Marking Knives and Scratch Awls

When doing precision layouts, such as defining the lines of an exposed joint, the best marking tools of all leave no mark of their own. Instead, they cut or emboss the wood fibers.

To lay out a line to a mark with absolute precision, I use a knife. Unlike a pencil mark, which has thickness of its own, the knife cuts a line only a thousandth of an inch wide.

In addition, the severed wood fibers form a shoulder against which to align the saw or chisel. This increases accuracy and it helps prevent tearout during the cutting process.

The accompanying photo shows a variety of marking knives and one scratch awl. Though the traditional wood handled tools are a joy to look at, I most often use the modern utility knife. The replaceable blades appeal to my reprehensibly lazy attitude toward sharpening, and their retractability prevents me from shredding my work apron.

Even when sharp, the scratch awl leaves behind a fuzzy, relatively wide line. I use it only when a marking knife won't do the job—such as when I'm attempting to mark a line parallel to the grain of the wood. In this situation, a knife won't leave a visible line. It may also insist on following the wood grain instead of the straight edge of a layout tool. Scratch awls usually ignore the run of the grain. In addition, they are irreplaceable for marking the centers of holes, as they simultaneously provide a pilot hole for the drill bit.

Tools to Measure Lengths

Probably the most common operation in the layout of any project is the measuring of lengths. With the stock milled to its finished thickness and width, I find that much of layout is based around the length dimension. I always want to know, for example, the overall length of the piece, how long to make the tenons of certain joints, and where to locate assembly and hardware positions along the component's length. To determine these things, I use a variety of store-bought and shop-made tools.

Tape measures and folding rules

The retracting steel tape measure has proven itself to be extremely effective in finding lengths. Still, several of my woodworking mentors argue that a steel tape lacks the consistent accuracy of the classic carpenter's wooden folding ruler. As an example, they cite the tape measure's inferior performance in taking inside measurements. It is true that inside measurements are difficult to read with a tape—you must mentally add the thickness of the body to the measurement. Also, if the "zero hook" of the tape is not working properly, the measurement will be thrown off. For me, however, a properly adjusted steel tape provides more than enough accuracy for the layout procedures I ask of it. Perhaps this is because when I want absolute accuracy I do not use a numerical measuring device of any kind. Instead, I use one of a variety of layout sticks.

When shopping for a steel tape, look for one with a "true zero hook" (the *L*-shaped hook at the beginning of the tape) that works properly. This hook serves two purposes: It anchors the tape at the starting edge of the object to be measured and it acts as a stop when using the tape to take an inside measurement. To perform both these functions with accuracy, the hook must move along slotted holes an amount exactly equal to the thickness of the hook itself. Before buying any tape measure, check out the operation of the zero hook with a combination square as shown in the photographs.

No tape, however, stays true forever. If the tape is dropped or otherwise abused, run this same test

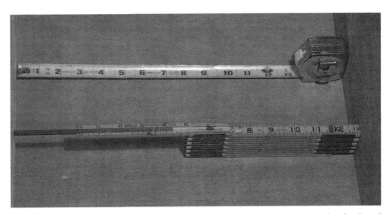

In taking a measurement between two surfaces, notice how the body of the steel tape measure gets in the way—the size of the case must be added to the visible measurement. The folding rule, however, offers a precise reading of the inside measurement along its integral brass extension rule.

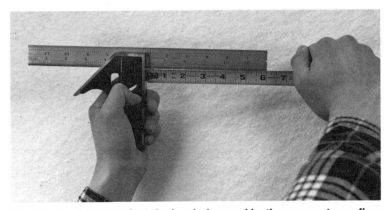

I hold a steel tape against the head of a combination square to confirm the accuracy of the rule when taking inside measurements. With the square's head set at 6″, the tape should read exactly 6″ at the end of the tongue.

To check to see if the true zero hook is working properly, I hook the end of the rule over the tongue and read the tape at the opposite end—it should be precisely 12″.

Measurement and Layout Tools **45**

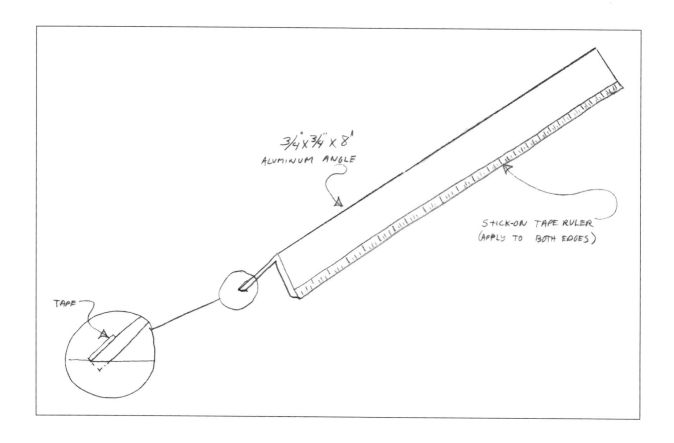

3/4" x 3/4" x 8" ALUMINUM ANGLE

STICK-ON TAPE RULER (APPLY TO BOTH EDGES)

TAPE

Shop-made 8′ straight-edge. *Grind a bevel on each edge so the outside edge touches the surface.*

to check the zeroing action. If it's off, adjust the tape back to true by slightly changing the hook angle with a pair of pliers. Also check to be sure that the slotted holes haven't become clogged with sawdust or rust. Finally, because some tapes go out of accuracy somewhere over their length, it is prudent to use the same tape measure throughout the entire layout of a specific project.

Straightedges

There is probably nothing more frustrating when testing a component assembly than not knowing when straight is really straight, or when flat is really flat. Therefore it's essential that there be a least one truly straight edge, at least 24″ to 36″ long, at hand in the shop. A straightedge will also be invaluable

when setting up woodworking machines to cut true to the lines, as we will discuss in chapter six.

A ruled straightedge is much handier to use than a tape measure when laying out marks on large surfaces, such as a sheet of plywood. Whenever I attempt to use a tape measure in this situation, the case of the tape is forever falling over, meaning I'm constantly forced to re-take my measurements. Also, the case conceals the last 2″ to 3″ of the tape reading, where Murphy's law predicts I'll have to make a mark. Although ruled straightedges of up to 8′ long are commercially available, you can make a far superior version with a length of aluminum angle iron and a couple of stick-on measuring tapes.

I also like to use a short-ruled

straightedge when measuring small distances, especially if I'm confronting critical dimensions measuring less than 1". In this situation, a tape measure is cumbersome and difficult to read. While you can use the ruled beam of a combination square, a straight rule with a hooked edge is more positive and is less likely to result in a misreading.

Another tool that comes in handy during certain layout procedures is the centering-rule straightedge. The measurements on this type of rule read away from either side of the center. To find a centerline between two fixed marks or edges, place the ruler on the marks in such a way that the same reading comes up to the right and to the left. The center point is then located at the zero measurement.

Story poles

The story pole is a simple shop-made, non-numerical measuring device that is very likely one of the most accurate and efficient methods known to woodworkers to transfer measurements from one place to another. Basically, it is a piece of wood on which marks are made to indicate specific dimensions of a form.

In general, I make the story pole from a square piece of wood so I can record up to four sets of dimensions. If I need only record one set, I make the story pole from a strip of ¼" plywood. When a lot of interrelated marks must be recorded (for example, when locating face frames and interior case panels) a story pole can be confusing. In this case, I divide a flat stick in half with a line and record the sets of dimensions to either side. Another type of story pole is the pinch stick—two sticks that slide

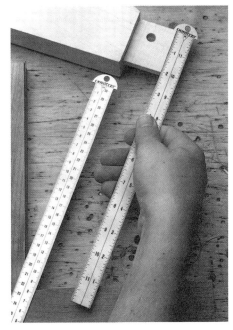

A hook built into a ruled straightedge provides a positive zero starting point. This speeds up measurement taking while decreasing the chance of errors.

Photograph courtesy of Veritas Tools, Inc.

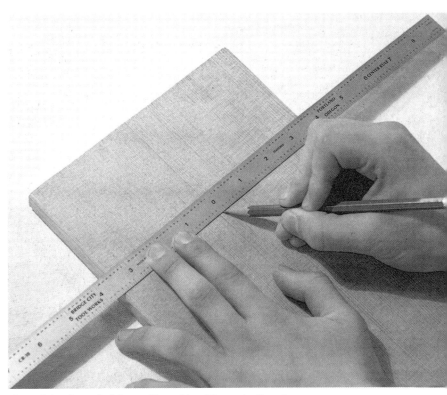

A straightedge ruled from either side of its centerline gives me an accurate and efficient way to lay out the center point of a board. To find the center, I adjust the ruler until the same dimension appears over each edge—the center point is then at the zero mark.

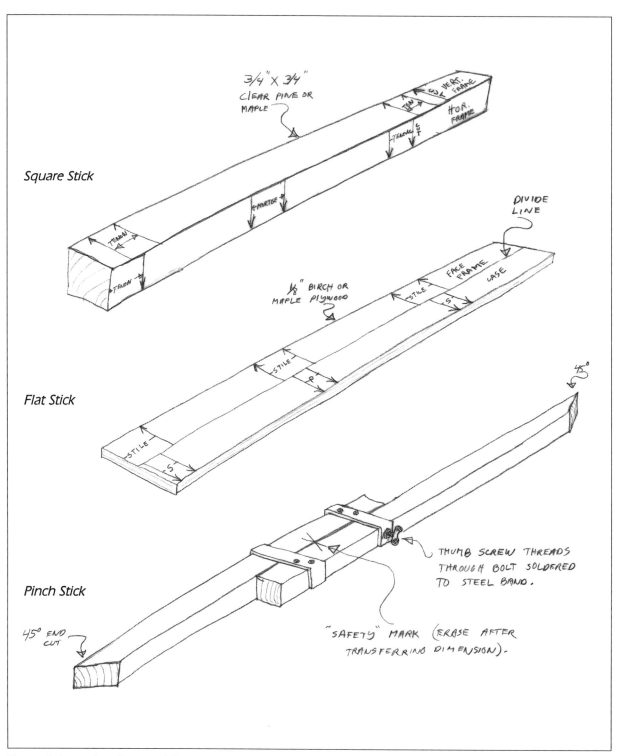

Square Stick

3/4" X 3/4" CLEAR PINE OR MAPLE

VERT. FRAME

HOR. FRAME

TENON CUT

TENON CUT

MORTISE

TENON

TENON

Flat Stick

1/8" BIRCH OR MAPLE PLYWOOD

DIVIDE LINE

FACE FRAME

STILE

CASE

STILE

P

STILE

S

STILE

S

45°

Pinch Stick

THUMB SCREW THREADS THROUGH BOLT SOLDERED TO STEEL BAND.

45° END CUT

"SAFETY" MARK (ERASE AFTER TRANSFERRING DIMENSION).

Types of story poles. Square stick: *can record dimensions of a structure on all four sides.* Flat stick: *shows relationship of components.* Pinch stick: *slides open until the ends index the width.*

by one another to record distances between two points.

To record dimensions on a story pole, work either from the measurements listed on the working drawings or, more desirably, from marks made by holding the stick against a full-scale drawing. Be sure to mark off the lengths of all the components, including joint cutlines, on the story pole. Always work from a clearly marked reference end of the stick. When using a pinch stick story pole, don't depend on the thumb screws to hold an accurate reading—make a light pencil mark across the sticks as an alignment check. In the next chapter, I'll show how to use the story pole to transfer the sizes of the various components to the stock.

Caliper and depth gauges

A vernier caliper is a precision instrument that is invaluable for determining precise inside and outside dimensions. I use it to gauge and transfer the dimensions of small components or parts of joints such as the thickness of a tenon. I also use it to find the inside dimensions of mortises and drill holes. Most calipers have a feeler bar for taking depth readings as well, though a gauge specially made for this purpose is more accurate and easier to read.

Whenever you can, try to use the gauge as a type of pinch stick. In this way, you can ignore the numerical reading all together, using the points on the tool to transfer the dimensions directly onto the work or to a marking gauge. This reduces the chance for mismeasurement, especially for people like me who can hardly remember their own phone numbers.

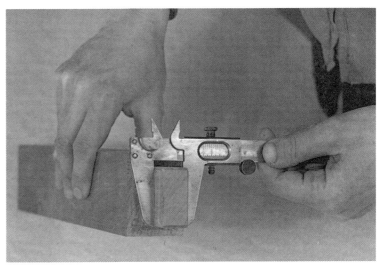

To determine the thickness of a tenon, I enclose it between the jaws of a vernier caliper. The caliper also tells me whether the tenon's faces are flat and parallel with one another.

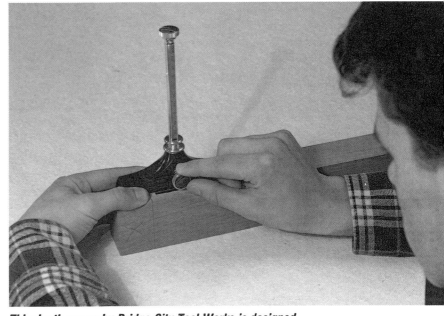

This depth gauge by Bridge City Tool Works is designed to measure depths of rabbets, dadoes and other types of joints and offsets. Here it is used to read the depth of a mortise. A cutting wheel fixed to the end of the readout sleeve allows you to transfer the depth dimension directly to the tenon stock.

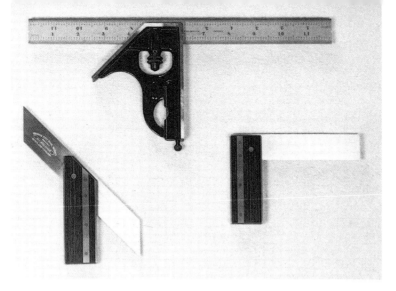

The blade of a try square is fixed precisely to the body of the tool at either a 45° or a 90° angle. A combination square also contains these fixed angles, though the head is free to slide along the blade, allowing the tongue to be used as an adjustable feeler gauge. Note how I've filed V-slots into the ends of the tongue — these allow me to use the tool as a pencil marking gauge.

Tools to Measure Angles

After the measuring of lengths, the next most common layout procedure is determining the angle to which a line is to be drawn. Much of the time this line is either a 90° or a 45° angle, easily marked with one of a number of types of squares. At other times I have to lay out cuts and assemblies at odd angles or a combination of angles. I'll determine these lines by using either bevel gauges in conjunction with a shop-made bevel board, or by using specialized measuring instruments.

Try squares and combination squares

While I've lately replaced my cubit stick with a steel rule tape measure, I still use essentially the same tool the Egyptians used for determining perpendiculars and 45° angles — a *try square*. I also use a carpenter's *framing square* for drawing out larger perpendiculars and other angled lines.

The *combination square* does the work of both the 45° and 90° try squares — and then some. Unlike try squares, which have fixed blades, a combination square's sliding head allows the tool to be used to transfer measurements as a height, depth and thickness gauge. To improve its use as a pencil marking gauge, I make a slight notch at the centerline at either end of the rule in which to fix a pencil point.

The ruled straightedge of the combination square is, of course, useful as a layout ruler for dimensions of less than 1'. My combination square has an optional decimal scale (the inches are broken down to hundredths of an inch) on one side of the rule, letting me lay out lengths by reading numbers directly off a calculator. This is handy for setting up other tools, such as a compass to describe a circle of a particular radius.

To maintain a combination square, keep the rule clean and coated with a light film of paraffin. (Don't use machine oil; it collects too much dust and it can stain the wood.) If the square is dropped, check it out using the procedure described below.

You can quickly and precisely test a 90° square for accuracy by holding it to a straightedge and drawing two lines — one with the body of the square oriented one way; the second with the body oriented in the opposite direction. Test the 45° try square and the 45° portion of the combination square by holding them to either side of a 45° to 45° drafting template. Adjust the try squares by honing the blades with a fine-toothed file. Move a framing square into true by hammering the metal at the corner of the square with a ball peen hammer — pounding near the outside corner spreads the metal and brings the legs of the square together; pounding at the inside corner has the opposite effect. If a combination square has gone out of square, do not attempt to fix it. Instead, send it back to the manufacturer for reconditioning.

Shop-made panel square

For laying out panels of up to 48", I use a panel square made from ½" hardwood plywood. In addition to providing full width layout lines on full sheets of plywood, this panel square serves me well as a template cutting guide that allows a router to true up the plywood's factory edge (as we'll discuss in chapter six). I tune up this panel square to true square by planing the stops, or adding sandpaper shims to them.

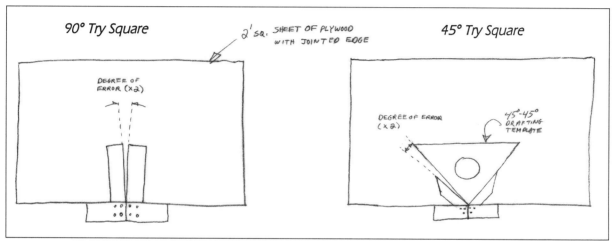

Checking a 90° try square. Step 1: *Hold the square tight to the edge and draw a line.* **Step 2:** *Reverse the square and draw a second line from the base of the first line. If the tool is square, the lines will overlap.*

Checking a 45° try square. *Hold the miter square to the edge and slide the template to it. Hold the template in place and reverse the square. If the tool is 45°, no gap appears between the template and the square.*

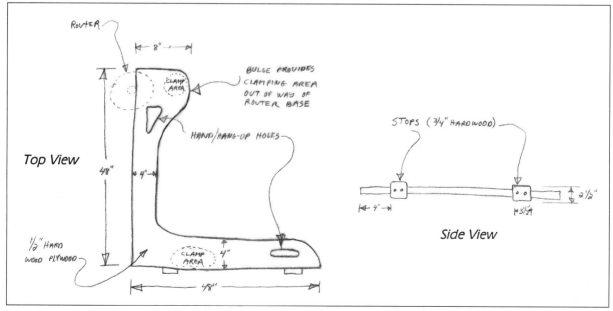

48″ panel square.

The infinitely adjustable and lockable blade(s) of a bevel gauge allows me to record and transfer the angle of any two intersecting surfaces. Note the boat builder's double-bladed gauge in the center of the picture—a useful tool for taking compound angles.

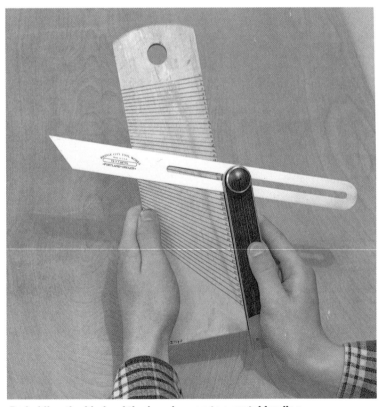

By holding the blade of the bevel gauge to a matching line marked across my shop-made bevel board, I can read out the degree of the recorded angle.

Bevel gauges

To determine angles other than 90° or 45°, the tool of choice is a bevel gauge, also sometimes called a *sliding T-bevel*. The thin-bladed version at left in the photograph is a Japanese model. I reach for it most often because of its long blade and the one-handed ease of setting and locking its blade to an angle. The antique bevel gauge has its lock at the end of the case, which means it requires the use of two hands.

The double-bladed gauge in the center is a boat builder's tool. Boat builders appreciate the presence of two blades on one tool because much of their work involves compound angles. With a double-bladed gauge, they can set both angles at once up on the boat, and then carry the information down to the workbench for layout onto the wood.

An immensely helpful companion to the bevel gauge is another boat builder's tool called a *bevel board*. This device is nothing more than a slab of wood with a set of lines drawn across it from 0° to 45°. I use the bevel board any time I'm measuring or laying down a series of different sized angles. With the leg of the bevel gauge held against the side of the board, I can quickly read (or set) the blade's angle. All I need do is hold the blade parallel to a marked angle line.

Angle measurement instruments

To find the bisecting angle of any given angle, you can either construct the bisector with a compass and straightedge (page 21), or you can use an *angle divider*. When the legs of this tool are made parallel with the angle lines, the inner arm automatically indicates the bisecting angle. When you hold this inner arm to the edge of a piece of wood, drawing a pencil along one leg then gives you the bisector.

Another use of the angle divider is to set angles to produce polygons. Most brands of these instruments have built-in settings for four-, five-, six-, eight-, and ten-sided figures.

Sometimes it's necessary to determine how to make the compound angles to produce pieces for projects with angled and miter-jointed sides (a planter box would be a good example). While you can take the angles from a full-scale drawing with a sequence of geometric steps, this is a rather complicated, time-consuming procedure. It's far easier to get the angles at which to set the tilt of the blade and the angle of the crosscut in the miter box by using a special circular ruler called an Angle-Ease. You just read the angle measurements directly from the ruler after dialing in the number of sides and the degree of tilt-out you desire. This ruler also helps you calculate how long to make the sides to reach a desired overall vertical height.

Tools to Lay Out Fixed Spaces

These tools are used to lay out lines or marks that must be spaced to certain and uniform distances. While you can do this work with a ruled straightedge and a marking tool of some kind, in almost every instance the specialized tools we'll cover here do the job more efficiently and with more accuracy.

The various marking gauges I describe next are all used to make straight lines. The compass scribe I describe later is used to transfer

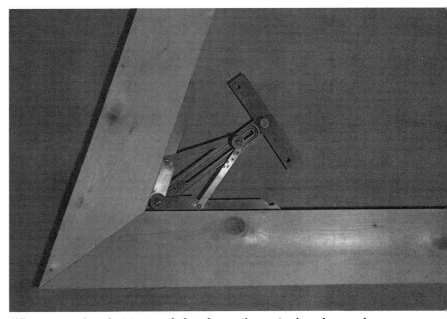

When pressed against two angled surfaces, the center leg of an angle divider tool automatically registers the bisecting angle. I can draw the bisector by holding the center leg to the edge of the stock and drawing a line against an outer leg.

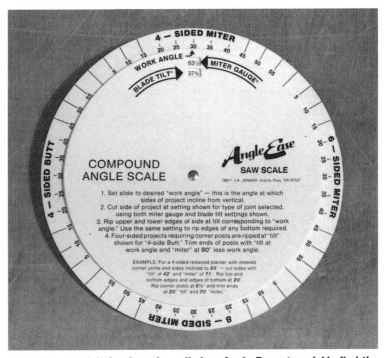

I use this special circular rule, called an Angle-Ease, to quickly find the degree at which to cut the joints of components that must meet at compound angles—the tool gives me a direct readout once I dial in the outline angles.

irregular lines to the work. I'll also show how to use dividers to space marks at fixed intervals.

Marking gauges

These tools make short work of laying out the cutlines of many kinds of joints. I also use them to mark the width or thickness to which a board is to be cut or planed. The most common gauge for laying out a line parallel to an edge consists of a block of wood (the "head") mounted on a stick (the "beam") into which a steel pin or knife blade has been set. A double-beam mortise gauge is used to lay out both sides of the mortise hole at the same time. The depth gauge shown in the center of the photograph also serves as a single-beam marking gauge.

While many antique American- and English-made marking gauges use a point rather than a knife to mark the wood, the modern gauges shown in the photograph (as well as most Japanese gauges), always use a knife. This knife makes a fine line that severs some of the wood fibers, which helps reduce tearout when making the actual cut. The steeply beveled edge of the knife also helps draw the tool's head tight against the edge of the wood as you run the tool along. If there were no bevel, the tool, and thus the mark, could easily wander.

You can make your own marking gauge featuring a knife marker and an optional pencil marker (for visibility in long rip cuts) during one or two pleasant evenings in your shop. Notice that the blade is tilted about 5° toward the back of the tool. This helps to keep the head tight to the board edge as you move the tool along. (If you are left-handed, build a mirror image of the gauge.)

When not in use, always bring the head of the gauge against the knife marker to protect it and keep it sharp. Lubricate the beam with

A marking gauge quickly and precisely lays out a line parallel to an edge at a fixed distance. With more than one beam, the gauge on the left can be set to mark two distances — useful for simultaneously laying out both sides of a mortise. These gauges by Bridge City Tool Works feature a cutting wheel that slices, rather than scratches, the layout lines.

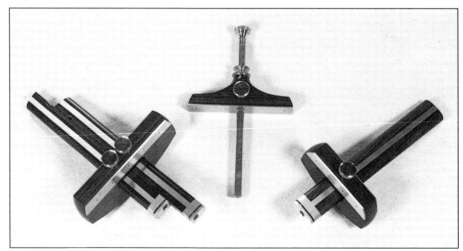

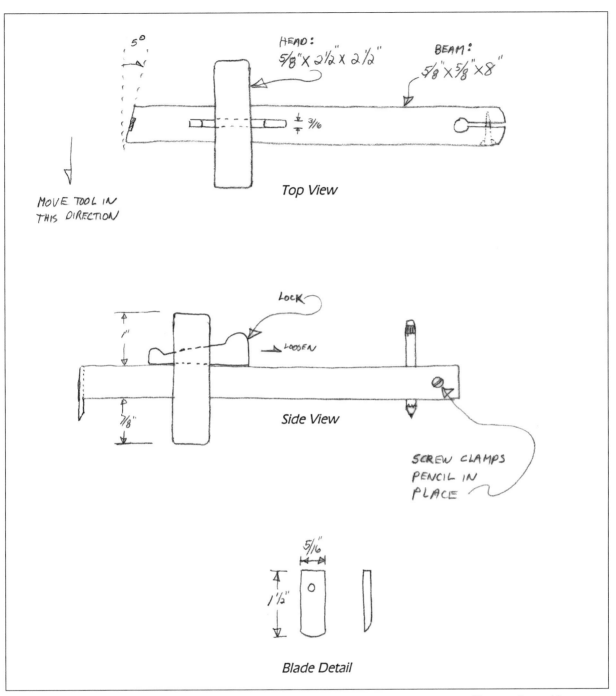

5°

HEAD:
5/8" X 2½" X 2½"

BEAM:
5/8" X 5/8" X 8"

⊥ 3/16"
T

Top View

MOVE TOOL IN
THIS DIRECTION

LOCK

LOOSEN

1"

7/8"

Side View

SCREW CLAMPS
PENCIL IN
PLACE

5/16"

1½"

O

Blade Detail

Shop-made marking gauge. Make all parts from a stable hardwood. Make the marking knife blade from a scrap of hacksaw blade.

Centerline marking gauge. Step 1: *Draw a centerline along the length of the stick and drill two holes for ⁵⁄₁₆″ dowels.* **Step 2:** *Install the dowels and use a small metal rule to draw parallel lines as shown. Mark the intersection points of the lines.* **Step 3:** *Connect the intersection points and mark the center where it crosses the centerline. Drill a hole here for a pencil.*

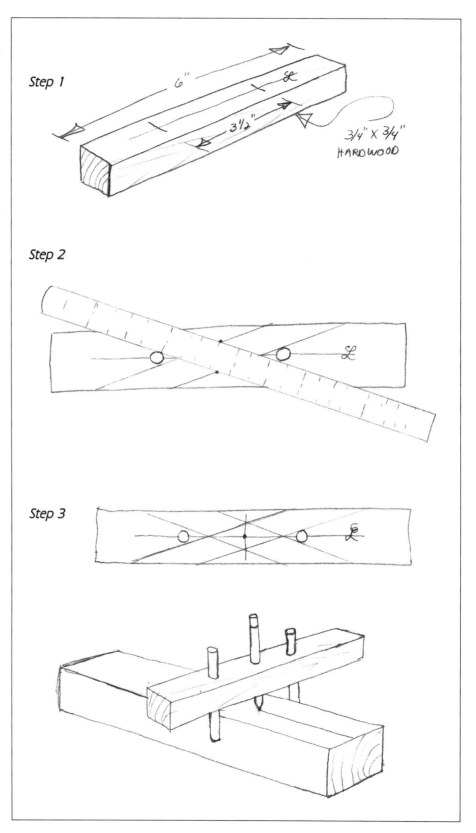

Step 1

6″

3½″

3/4″ X 3/4″
HARDWOOD

Step 2

Step 3

paraffin from the stub of a candle.

Centerline marking gauge

While you can use a regular marking gauge to run a line along the center of a width of board, a specialized *centerline marking gauge* will generally do the work more quickly and accurately. Its best feature, however, is its ability to automatically center itself, even on a tapered piece of wood.

To mark a centerline, lay the gauge across the stock and angle the beam until both dowels bear against opposite edges of the board. The center marker is now automatically located on the centerline of the board. Run the gauge along the length of the stock, being sure to keep the dowels bearing on the edges. I generally prefer to use a pencil marker because a knife edge doesn't show up well when run along the grain of the wood.

Compass scribes and dividers

Besides the obvious use of a compass scribe to draw circles to an infinite variety of radii (easier done than said!), it is also indispensable as a specialized marking gauge. Whenever I need to copy an irregular curve or tapered line onto the work (a common task when fitting a built-in project or when cope-jointing moldings), I use a compass scribe to mark the cutline.

Do not make the mistake of using your drafting compass for layout work. The rigors of marking on wood can quickly destroy these delicate instruments. Instead, use a rugged version of the compass, commonly available at hardware stores.

I use a set of dividers (a compass with two pins) whenever I need to step out equal spaces along the length of a narrow component. To ensure accuracy during layout, keep the points of the legs sharp to prevent slipping.

Tools to Lay Out Curves

Project layouts, like life, would be much simpler if curves weren't thrown into the process, but neither would be as interesting. With the proper tools, laying out curves is neither difficult nor particularly time-consuming. In fact, I think it's one of the more fun layout jobs.

Compasses and trammel points

These tools help you deal with curves of fixed radii. Small arcs and circles are easily drawn with a compass and pencil. Larger radii curves that fall out of the range of your compass can be drawn with a set of trammel points mounted on a beam. While these points are widely available through tool suppliers, I prefer my shop-made version. Since the sliding pencil marker head and the pivot point are permanently attached to the beam, I find my version is quicker and easier to set up and put to use.

Adjustable battens to fair irregular curves

An irregular curve is any line that is constructed from more than one radius along its length. While smaller irregular curves can sometimes be taken care of with ship's curves, larger curves need to be drawn to *fairing battens*.

These battens need be nothing more than a square section of clear, straight-grained wood cut about 1' longer than the maximum length of the curve. Be aware that the smaller

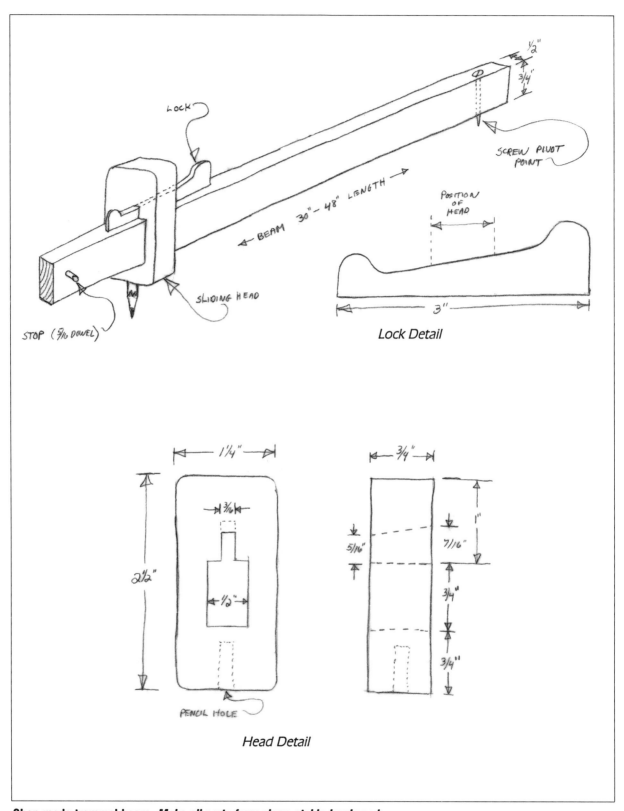

LOCK

SCREW PIVOT POINT

BEAM 30" – 48" LENGTH

SLIDING HEAD

STOP (5/16 DOWEL)

1/2"

3/4"

POSITION OF HEAD

3"

Lock Detail

1 1/4"

3/16"

2 1/2"

1/2"

PENCIL HOLE

3/4"

5/16"

1"

7/16"

3/4"

3/4"

Head Detail

Shop-made trammel beam. *Make all parts from clear, stable hardwood.*

the cross section of the batten, the tighter the curve it can take without breaking. For radii of greater than 2' or 3', I find a ⅜" square cross section is fine. Down to 1', a ¼" batten usually works.

In use, the batten is held in place to the station points of the curve with tacks or small lead weights. Never drive a tack through the batten — this can throw the curve out of fair. Even worse, you might split the thin batten stock.

Now that we've looked at the variety of measurement and layout tools available for getting the lines down onto the wood, it's time to get our hands on them. In the next chapter, I'll go over many of the standard procedures for working with these devices. In addition, I'll introduce you to some tricks for laying out cutlines in difficult and unusual situations.

Chapter 5
The Layout Process: Down to the Lines

N ow it's time to transform your paperwork into woodwork. Good drawings, carefully double-checked, should have produced clear and accurate cutlists. And with good cutlists, all that stands between you and the wood ready to cut and assemble is the laying down of the lines.

Layout begins with defining the rough overall dimensions of all the component pieces of the project. As the process continues, you commit the pieces to their exact dimensions, usually working from the largest toward the smallest. With both the solid wood and panel stock components cut to size, any curves, rounded corners or other details called for by the design are laid out. Then, usually through the use of story poles, joint lines and part assembly positions are located and marked out. The components are then ready to be cut, tried, trued and assembled.

Laying Out Boards to Rough Width and Length

In chapter three, I showed you how to compile and organize the master cutlists for solid and panel stock. From these lists, graphic picture boards are made to represent the layout of the component pieces on the stock. But while these graphics are invaluable for puzzling out the most efficient layout of boards and panel stock, I don't always use them.

Unlike uniform manufactured panels, solid wood stock typically contains knots, cracks, curved edges, unattractive grain patterns and a host of other defects. To produce a realistic layout, all these must be accounted for in the graphic representation of the board.

A timber crayon clearly defines the rough widths and lengths of some furniture components on a set of boards. Note that waste areas have been marked with an X — this indicates which side of the line the saw should be run to.

Because of this, I rarely create picture board graphics for solid stock if there are more than three or four boards involved in the project. Even though it's definitely more strenuous to juggle the puzzle with solid boards rather than slips of paper, I've discovered it's actually less troublesome to go directly from the cutlist to the wood itself.

Because many of the cutting procedures require that a face or an edge of the board act as a reference against a table or fence, you must first true these. Surface both faces of the board flat and to a uniform thickness (unless, of course, a taper is specified). Use the winding sticks shown in chapter four to check for twist. Later, when cutting the components out of the stock, be sure to make the edges parallel to one another and to joint them straight.

Before laying out the cuts, in-

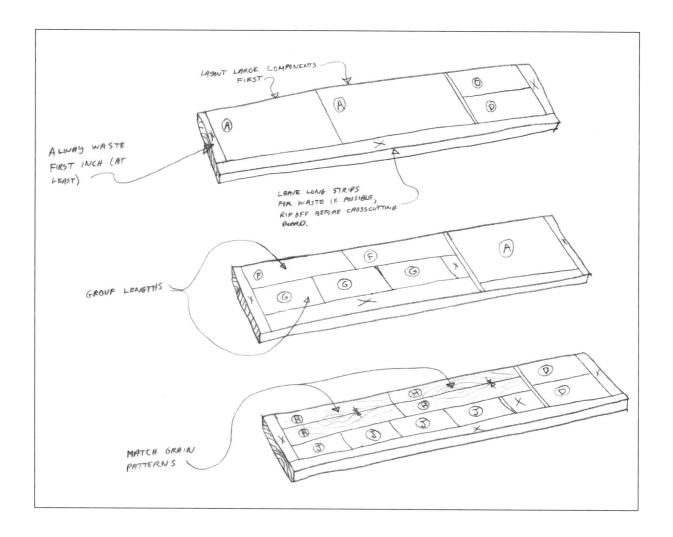

Board layout examples.

spect the boards for defects. With a piece of chalk or a timber crayon, mark out any areas that cannot be used. Be sure to look at both sides. Even if you can't see them, the ends of mill-length boards nearly always contain drying checks. Play it safe and waste the first and last inch.

Begin layout by locating the largest pieces on the largest boards. Allow at least 1″ extra in length for the rough cut, marking the kerf between pieces with a double line. To reduce waste, lay out long pieces on boards with relatively straight edges; reserve short pieces for the boards with the most curve. With a

straightedge or chalk line, mark long components at least ⅛″ over-width to provide room to rejoin them straight to the final width. If the stock is reactive, curving as it is ripped, you will either have to provide a larger allowance of over-width, or select a more stable board for long components.

As you work your way down to the smallest pieces, try to leave long strips as waste rather than short, wide pieces, which almost never find a use. Also try to group lengths so that the boards can be crosscut prior to ripping. Finally, be aware of components that must have matching grain patterns, such as meeting stiles on a pair of door frames. Lay these out side by side, taking the time to find pleasing grain patterns.

The most efficient, precise method for laying out final dimension lines (and joint and assembly position marks as well) is with a story pole. Mark the component lengths and widths on the story pole, clamp the stick to the rough cut pieces, and transfer the marks to the stock.

Laying Out Panel Stock

Unless you are using shop-grade panel stock (which may contain significant defects), you need only quickly examine the panels for shipping damage before transferring the layout from the graphic picture boards. If the stock is hardwood plywood with sides of different grades, be sure to lay out on the better side.

The way I do a panel stock layout depends on how I intend to make the cuts. If I'll be using a table saw setup for panel sizing (see the next chapter), I only rough in the location of the pieces with chalk lines. Referring to the picture board, I mark the approximate location of the kerfs, write in the dimensions, and label the components with the appropriate symbols. All the cuts are then made by setting the fence of the table saw (and, for some cuts, the stop on the radial arm saw) to the dimensions chalked on the panel.

Without the benefit of a panel sizing table saw setup, you must lay out exact cutlines on the panel stock. Begin by laying out the marks with a long, ruled straightedge. First draw out any full-length rip cut in the panel. If there isn't a full-length

rip, lay out the largest component instead.

Now rip the panel along the line or cut out the largest component. (I'll cover the details of making precise hand-powered cuts on panel stock in the next chapter.) Lay out, then cut out, one component at a time. Using a tape measure or story pole with the large panel square, lay out the crosscuts. Remember to first set the knife to the mark, and then slide the square or straightedge against the blade. To ensure a straight line, keep the blade tight to the base of the square or straightedge. If the knife line is hard to see, either darken it with a sharp, hard lead (4H) drafting pencil, or lighten it by rubbing in powdered white chalk.

Laying out a panel with a true 45° angle

Occasionally it's necessary to lay out a wide component with a true 45°

Once the pieces have been rough cut from the boards, I use a story pole to transfer the final cutting dimensions from the full-scale drawing. I hold the story pole securely to the stock to prevent the pole from slipping and producing a false layout line.

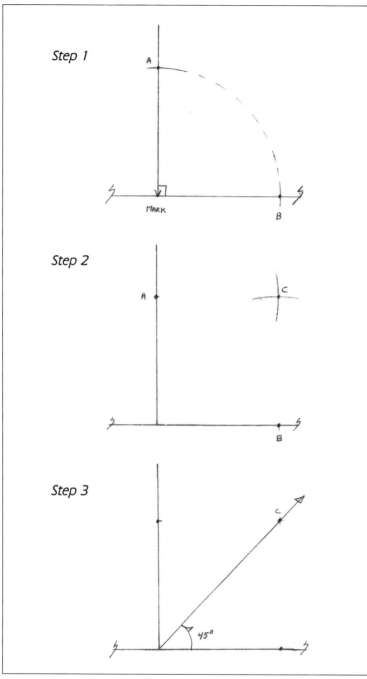

Step 1

A

MARK

B

Step 2

A

C

B

Step 3

C

45°

Construction of a large 45° angle. Step 1: *Erect a perpendicular from the starting mark, and then swing the trammel beam to create points* **A** *and* **B.** *(The larger the arc, the more accurate the line.)* **Step 2:** *Set the point of the beam at* **A,** *and then* **B;** *swing arcs to create an intersection at point* **C. Step 3:** *Draw a line through* **C** *from the starting mark.*

angle along one side. While you can easily find this angle by laying a framing square across the edge and aligning it to the same measurement on either leg, the span is rather short. To ensure accuracy, use geometry to establish the angle over a long length.

In the accompanying drawing, the trammel beam swings an arc through a line erected perpendicular to the end mark and down to a side. The trammel beam is then pivoted from each mark at the same radius, creating an intersection point. The line drawn from the end mark to this intersection forms a perfect 45° angle with the side of the component.

Laying Out Curves and Rounded Corners

I like this part of the layout process. Swinging large, single-radius curves with a trammel beam, or setting up battens to fair in irregular curves, is exhilarating after pushing a marking knife or pencil along a straightedge for what seems like miles. Even the simple task of drawing in a rounded corner gives me a little thrill. Perhaps this is due to the feeling that I'm getting close to seeing the pieces drawn out to their final shape.

The simplest way to swing a curved layout line with a single radius is with a trammel beam. The only real trick to using the tool is finding where to place the pivot point. It is almost always necessary to create that place, as it invariably occurs somewhere off the board on which the curve is being drawn. In the photograph above right you can see how I have temporarily tacked down an extension board perpendicular to the edge of the board

With the point of a trammel beam set on a pivot point established on a board temporarily held to the stock, the pencil marker swings an arch between predetermined points along the edge of the board.

Finding the pivot point for a trammel beam. Step 1: *Set an extension board between* A *and* B *marks. Erect a centerline perpendicular by swinging arcs above and below the edge of the board.* **Step 2:** *Connect a line from height center point* C *to* B. *Swing arcs to erect a perpendicular centerline. Mark* D *where this line intersects the first perpendicular.* **Step 3:** *Set the beam's pivot point on* D, *and the pencil on* A. *Swing an arc to* B.

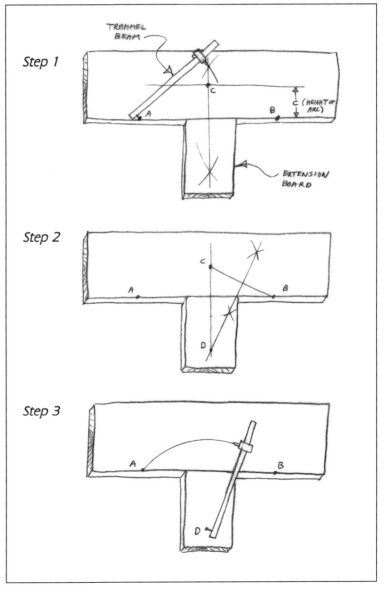

that's receiving the curve.

This drawing at right shows how to find the pivot point on the extension board. It is assumed that you know the end points of the curve along the edge of the board (points *A* and *B* in the drawing) and that you know the maximum height the curve will achieve between them (point *C*).

To find the center of the circle whose circumference passes through these three points, first erect a perpendicular at the centerline between points *A* and *B*. To do this, swing an arc set to a radius somewhat greater than half the distance between the two marks and make intersection points above and below the edge of the board. Connecting these points creates a perpendicular centerline that passes

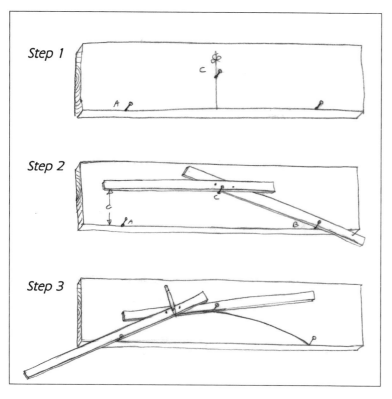

Step 1

Step 2

Step 3

Stick method for drawing large radius arches. Step 1: *Set nails at the ends of the arc along the edge of the board and at the point of maximum height along the centerline of the arc. Step 2: Select two sticks with parallel edges. Place the first stick on a line from C to B. Place the second along the C height line (parallel to the board's edge). Tack or screw them together. Step 3: Place a pencil at the inside juncture of the sticks and slide the stick assembly along the nails.*

an old boat builder's trick for laying out arched deck beams. Like most old-time tricks, it's somewhat primitive, but wholly adequate to perform the task.

Begin by nailing two sticks together as shown in the drawing. Set nails at the appropriate points and then draw the arch by placing a pencil at the inside intersection of the sticks and then moving the assembly so that the intersection carries from point A to point B. If you've kept the inside edges of the sticks tight against the nails, you should leave behind a perfect arc.

Laying out an ellipse

On many projects, an arch can look much more dramatic as a portion of an ellipse rather than a portion of a circle. Using a simple jig with a framing square helps make the drawing of an ellipse almost as simple as swinging a circle.

To produce the ellipse, first decide where you wish the center point of the form to be. Then establish the height and length of the ellipse along a vertical and a horizontal axis intersecting this point. The next step is to get out a $3/4'' \times 3/4''$ stick about $1\frac{1}{2}''$ longer than the distance between the center of the ellipse (C) and point A (see the drawing at right). Locate and drill three holes in the stick as shown. Insert dowels in the first two holes and a pencil in the other.

To draw in the form, align a framing square with the two axes, securing it with double-sided carpet tape. Holding the stick's dowels firmly and consistently against the square, describe one quadrant of the ellipse with the pencil. Move the square to draw the other quadrants.

though the middle of the circle.

Now draw a straight line between C and B and, using the same process outlined above, erect a perpendicular at CB's center point. You'll find the center point of the circle (point D) where this centerline intersects the centerline created between A and B. Set the trammel beam pivot on point D and swing an arc through A, C and B. A little adjustment to the location of the pivot point may be necessary to get it perfect.

Stick method for drawing a large, single-radius curve

Occasionally, you may be confronted by curves that are too large to comfortably lay out with a trammel beam (since one hand must hold the pivot in place while the other controls the pencil). The solution is

Drawing irregular curves to a batten

My definition of an irregular curve is a curve that is drawn to more than one radius point. If the curve involves only one or two different radii, an easy and effective way to draw it is to swing connecting arcs using a compass or trammel beam. If the curve is constantly changing radii, use french curves as drawing templates. For more complex or larger curves, especially when the radii might not be specified on the plans, draw in the curve with either an adjustable curve or with a wooden batten. The adjustable curve or batten is set to a series of points, or *stations*, that you establish as places through which the curve must pass. The more complex the curve, the more stations are necessary to accurately define it.

To determine the stations, go to either the scaled or the full-size working drawings on which the curve appears, and draw a grid around the curve (see page 37). Then draw the grid on the wood. Measure where the curve intersects the lines of the grid on the drawing, and transfer these points to the grid on the wood. These are the station points for the curve.

The photo above shows me drawing in the arched top of a bed headboard. Note how I have sprung a wood batten to touch nails set at the station points. Also notice the scrap boards screwed to the bench at either end of the headboard, which provide a place to fix the ends of the batten with nails. If the ends were allowed to hang free, the curve would tend to straighten out near its extremities. This, in turn, would make the curve go out of fair be-

A long, smooth curve results from drawing a line to a flexible wooden batten. Temporarily secure the batten to the station points established by reading measurements from a scaled grid on the working drawing.

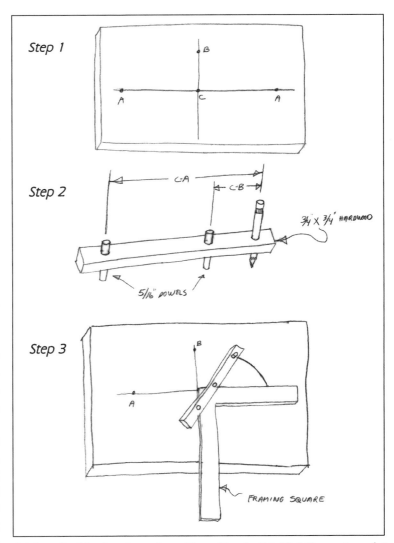

Stick method for drawing out an ellipse. Step 1: *Establish the center point of the ellipse and draw a horizontal and a vertical axis. Mark* **A** *and* **B** *points.* **Step 2:** *Make a marking gauge from a stick, placing dowels and a pencil as shown. Make the stick 1½" longer than distance* **C-A.** **Step 3:** *Lay a framing square in a quadrant of the axis and run the dowels of the gauge against the leg and tongue. Mark the ellipse with the pencil. Flip the square to other quadrants to complete the ellipse.*

tween the station points.

Sight along the length of the batten to check for fairness before drawing in the line. Always go with what looks right to your eye; don't hesitate to overrule a station point if necessary to get a fair curve.

Laying out curves to templates

If a project requires a number of components to be cut to a similar curve, you'll save time by making up a template to the exact dimensions of the component. I like to use ⅛" plywood doorskin for template stock because it is stiff and stable (unlike poster board or Mylar), and because I can shape it precisely to dimension with rasps and hand planes.

To make the template, use the grid method outlined above to establish the curve's station points on the template stock, and then draw it in with adjustable curves, battens or french curve templates. If the template is small, you can use vellum or Mylar traced from the full-scale drawing as I discussed in chapter three. Carefully fair the template with hand tools.

Laying out rounded corners

In chapter two, I introduced you to a series of drafting methods for creating an arc between two lines. When working on three-dimensional solid wood rather than two-dimensional paper, it is quicker to locate and draw out the arcs with a marking gauge followed by a compass scribe. Whether the lines meet perpendicularly, or at an acute or obtuse angle, the method remains the same.

To find where to place the compass point to draw in the arc, you must first decide what radius you wish the arc to be. If this has not already been specified on your working drawings, you can eyeball a variety of radii until one looks right by holding a selection of jar lids or other circular objects in the approximate position.

Having selected an arc, set a marking gauge (preferably a pencil marking gauge to avoid scratching the wood) to the arc's radius, and

Here an arched table apron is reproduced from a template made from ⅛" plywood doorskin. Applying double-faced carpet tape to the back of the template prevents its slipping and throwing off the layout.

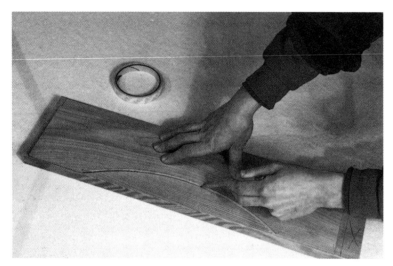

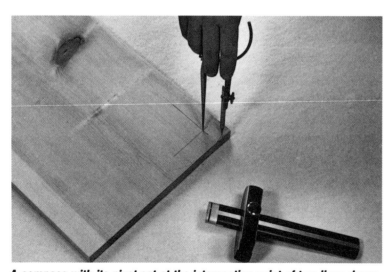

A compass with its pivot set at the intersection point of two lines draws in a rounded corner. The intersecting lines were established with a marking gauge set to the radius of the corner.

make a line parallel with each leg of the angle. Set a compass scribe to the radius, fix the point where the lines intersect, and then swing the arc.

There's no need to bother with any of this if the rounded corner is relatively small. In this case use coins as templates: A penny produces a ⅜″ radius arc; a quarter equals about a ½″ arc; and a half-dollar produces a ⅝″ arc.

Techniques for Laying Out Equal Divisions

As the layout proceeds from the defining of overall dimensions toward the more intricate laying out of joint lines and assembly positions, there is often the need to divide widths and lengths into equal parts. Centerlines along the length of a board must be found to locate assembly positions and joints. Repetitive joints such as dovetails require you to divide a board equally into the number of tails you wish to create. Components that are to be located evenly between two points, such as chair slats, must be laid out so they end up with equal spacings between them.

Luckily, there are layout tools and techniques to help you do most of these tasks without having to crunch any numbers. For me, anyway, that means these layouts go quickly and accurately.

To run a centerline down the length of a board, use the center marking device introduced in the last chapter. Be sure to keep the gauge's dowels tight to either side of the board as you draw the centerline with the pencil marker. You can also use a standard marking gauge to mark a centerline once you know where to set the blade or pencil. To

Step 1

MARKING GAUGE

STOCK

Step 2

Step 3

(Left) *Using a marking gauge to find a centerline.* **Step 1:** *Set the gauge by eye to an approximation of the centerline. Draw a short line (about 1″).* **Step 2:** *Bring the head of the gauge over to the opposite edge and, without changing the setting, draw a second line.* **Step 3:** *If the first line was dead-on center, the second line should fall atop it. Otherwise, the centerline is located precisely between the two lines.*

(Below) *With a ruler set across a board, I can lay out the width of the board into equal divisions. I fix the zero on one side of the rule over one edge and a number equal to the desired number of divisions over the other edge. I mark the division lines at the whole numbers.*

quickly find this center point, follow the steps in the drawing.

You can use an ordinary ruled straightedge to divide the width of a board into any number of parts. It's easy. Simply lay the ruler across the board so that one end of the rule (zero) touches one edge. Now orient the rule so that the number indicating the number of divisions you wish to make on the board touches the opposite edge. You will very likely have to angle the rule to get the numbers to line up.

Spacing components between two points

Things get a little more complicated if components are to be laid out be-

Spacing components between two points. *Spacing components between two points does not result in equal gaps if the components are centered on equal division lines. To create equal gaps, use the following formulas to find centerlines.*

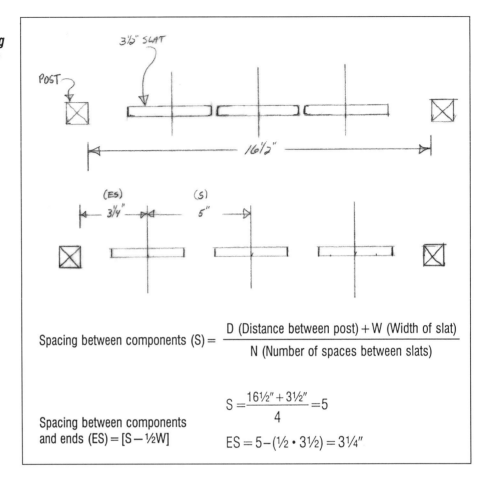

Spacing between components (S) = $\dfrac{\text{D (Distance between post)} + \text{W (Width of slat)}}{\text{N (Number of spaces between slats)}}$

Spacing between components and ends (ES) = [S − ½W]

$$S = \frac{16½'' + 3½''}{4} = 5$$

$$ES = 5 - (½ \cdot 3½) = 3¼''$$

tween two points. Because they have width of their own, the components cannot be centered over equal division lines established as previously described. If you did so, the spaces between the components themselves would be equal, but not between the outside components and the end marks. The upper portion of the drawing of a chair's vertical back slats laid out between two posts shows why this happens.

To lay out the centerlines to evenly space components between two points, refer to the example in the drawing and follow this procedure:

1. Measure the distance between the posts (16½").

2. Add to this measurement the width (3½") of one back slat (16½" + 3½" = 20").

3. Divide this sum by the number of spaces (four) between the slats: (20"/4 = 5").

4. To lay out the centerlines of the outside slats, measure over from each post 5" minus half the width (1¾") of a slat (5"−1¾" = 3¼") and make a mark.

5. Lay out the centerlines of the inner slats at 5" centers from these points.

After determining the diameter of the circle you wish to divide, use the chart provided to divide the circle into three to one hundred spaces. For example, if you wish to divide

Dividing circles and irregular curves into equal parts
Circle division table

To divide a circle into equal parts, find the number of divisions desired in the left-hand column. The right-hand column shows the length to set the divider to step out the divisions along the perimeter of the circle. *Note:* These figures are for a 1″ diameter circle. For other sizes, multiply the length of chord by the diameter of the circle desired.

No. of spaces	Length of chord	No. of spaces	Length of chord	No. of spaces	Length of chord	No. of spaces	Length of chord	No. of spaces	Length of chord
3	0.8660	23	0.1362	43	0.0730	63	0.0499	83	0.0378
4	0.7071	24	0.1305	44	0.0713	64	0.0491	84	0.0374
5	0.5878	25	0.1253	45	0.0698	65	0.0483	85	0.0370
6	0.5000	26	0.1205	46	0.0682	66	0.0476	86	0.0365
7	0.4339	27	0.1161	47	0.0668	67	0.0469	87	0.0361
8	0.3827	28	0.1120	48	0.0654	68	0.0462	88	0.0357
9	0.3420	29	0.1081	49	0.0641	69	0.0455	89	0.0353
10	0.3090	30	0.1045	50	0.0628	70	0.0449	90	0.0349
11	0.2818	31	0.1012	51	0.0616	71	0.0442	91	0.0345
12	0.2588	32	0.0980	52	0.0604	72	0.0436	92	0.0341
13	0.2393	33	0.0951	53	0.0592	73	0.0430	93	0.0338
14	0.2224	34	0.0923	54	0.0581	74	0.0424	94	0.0334
15	0.2079	35	0.0896	55	0.0571	75	0.0419	95	0.0331
16	0.1951	36	0.0872	56	0.0561	76	0.0413	96	0.0327
17	0.1837	37	0.0848	57	0.0551	77	0.0408	97	0.0324
18	0.1736	38	0.0826	58	0.0541	78	0.0403	98	0.0321
19	0.1645	39	0.0805	59	0.0532	79	0.0398	99	0.0317
20	0.1564	40	0.0785	60	0.0523	80	0.0393	100	0.0314
21	0.1490	41	0.0765	61	0.0515	81	0.388		
22	0.1423	42	0.0747	62	0.0507	82	0.383		

a 16″ diameter circle into six even parts, look up the chord length at six spaces: 0.500. Multiply this decimal fraction by 16″ to yield 8″. Now set a pair of dividers to 8″.

I find a combination square very useful for setting divider leg spans. You can fix the points into the engraved rule marks, ensuring high accuracy. This also prevents the points from slipping as you lock the divider down. If you set the first point on the 1″ line, remember to add this inch to the measurement for setting the other leg. To mark out even spaces, step the divider around the circumference of the circle. If the tool has been set correctly, the last mark should coincide with the starting mark.

If necessary, you can easily find the diameter of a circle with a carpenter's framing square. Place the outside corner of the square to the inner circumference of the circle. Then orient the legs so they read equal lengths where they cross the circle. Connect these intersections

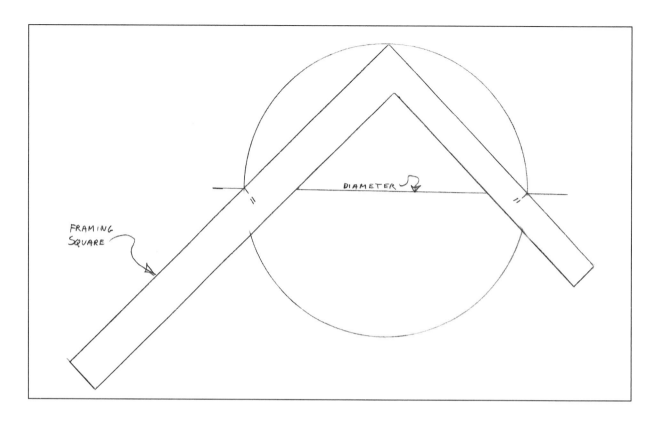

DIAMETER

FRAMING SQUARE

Finding the diameter of a circle with a framing square. *To find the diameter of a circle, set a square in the circle with its corners touching the circle's perimeter. Orient the square so that the same measurement appears on each leg of the square where it crosses the circle. A line connecting these points is the diameter of the circle.*

with a straight line: This is the diameter of the circle.

Laying out polygons

Laying out polygons on wood is done with just one woodworking tool: a framing square to which a pair of straight sticks have been clamped.

The polygon layout table provided shows where to set this stick along the body and tongue of the square to draw the facet angle of a variety of polygons. In the accompanying photograph, I am laying out a hexagon-shaped table surface on a square-ended blank. Note that I'm holding the stick tight along one side of the blank as I draw the facet angle along the tongue. Because the stick has been paired to another one below the square, I can simply flip the square over if I want to draw the

facet on the opposite side.

Laying out a hexagon along a length

When a length of stock must be made round, the first step in the procedure is to lay it out to be cut into a hexagonal cross section. This is true whether the stock is to be rounded on a lathe or by a series of hand tools.

Lay out the facet points of a hexagonal cross section along a length of stock using a marking gauge. To do this, first mill out the piece perfectly square in cross section. Then draw diagonals on the end of the stock from corner to corner. Set the marking gauge to the distance between a corner and the intersection of these lines. Now run the gauge the full length of the squared blank, marking one facet point. Continue

Number of Sides	Position of Stick on Framing Square	
	TONGUE (Short Leg)	BODY (Long Leg)
3	12″	20⅞″
4	12″	12″
5	12″	8²⁵⁄₃₂″
6	12″	6¹⁵⁄₁₆″
8	12″	4³¹⁄₃₂″
12	12″	3⁷⁄₃₂″

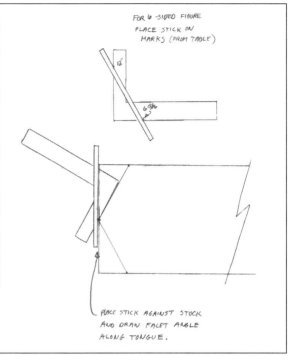

FOR 6-SIDED FIGURE PLACE STICK ON MARKS (FROM TABLE)

12″

6¹⁵⁄₁₆

PLACE STICK AGAINST STOCK AND DRAW FACET ANGLE ALONG TONGUE.

Polygon layout table for setting up a framing square.

The facets of an octagon are drawn onto a piece of stock using a framing square as a marking guide. I secure a pair of sticks to the square at the measurements indicated by the polygon layout table—the sticks jig the square against the stock.

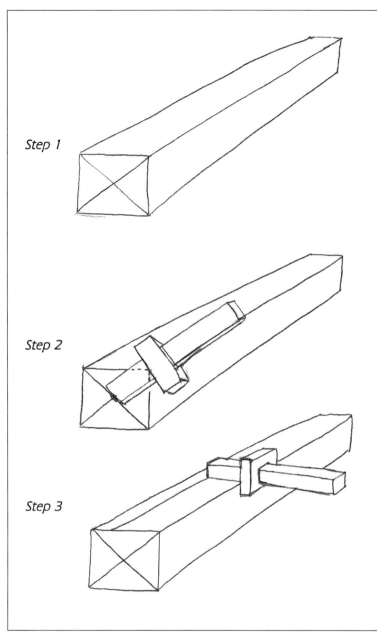

Layout of a hexagon along a length of stock. **Step 1:** *Draw diagonal lines across the end of a squared length of wood.* **Step 2:** *Set the marking gauge so the head touches the corner of the stock while the marker touches the intersection of the diagonals.* **Step 3:** *Run the marking gauge along the stock at this setting. Repeat at all eight facet points.*

around the stock until all eight points are marked.

Laying Out Joint Lines

Because the layout of joint lines (and also assembly position points) is so crucial to the final outcome of any project, this is the time to be especially careful with your measuring and layout techniques. Bear with me for a moment while I review some points made earlier:

■ Be sure to hold the tape measure, ruled straightedge or story pole tight to the work to eliminate parallax when sighting the marks against the lines. Use spring clamps if necessary to prevent slipping.

■ Make the marks with either a *V* tick mark from a sharp, hard pencil, or with a knife cut.

■ If using taped or ruled dimensions to lay out a series of lengths, never step out the dimensions from one point to another. Doing so invariably causes the layout to "grow." Though it means crunching numbers, always measure out from one reference point.

■ When using a square, bevel gauge or straightedge to run out a line from a mark, always place the pencil or knife on the mark first, and then slide the tool to it.

In the following sections, I'll introduce you to a series of techniques for laying out a variety of common joints. You should be able to apply the basic principles of these techniques to lay out nearly any other kind of woodworking joint.

Laying out a lap joint

To lay out a lap joint, you must first know exactly where the shoulders of the joints are to appear on both components. Either read the dimensions from the plans or, better, mark a story pole directly off the full-scale drawing. Also determine the overall length of the components (if the stock has not already been final cut to length). Transfer the shoulder and overall length marks to the stock with a knife cut. The pieces should already be sized to their final thickness and width and marked with part and orientation symbols matching those shown in your working drawing.

With the knife held to a combination or try square, cut a line all the way around the stock at the overall length marks. Move the knife to the shoulder mark and cut a line square across. Repeat this on the other piece, paying attention to the orientation marks and to the X marks indicating the waste side of the cut. The shoulder cuts must be on opposing faces.

The next step is to define the depth of the lap joint. Set a marking gauge to the centerline of the thickness of the stock as shown earlier in this chapter. Then place the gauge's head firmly to the surface of the stock marked with the X (indicating the waste side of the lap joint), and run the tool around the end of the stock. The bevel of the marking cutter should be facing the waste side of the cut. In hard woods, take mul-

A view of two unassembled joints: *A mortise-and-tenon joint is shown at the rear of the picture and a lap joint toward the front.*

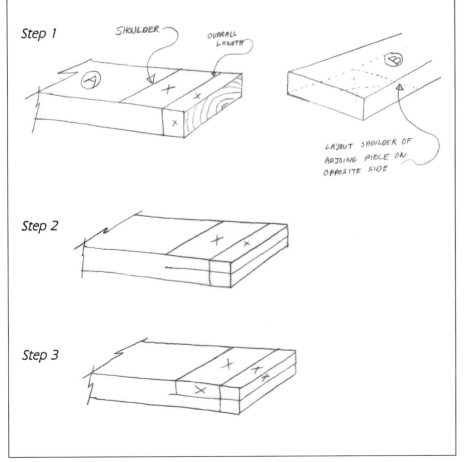

Layout of a lap joint. Step 1: *Lay out the overall length and the shoulder cutline with a marking knife.* **Step 2:** *Use a marking gauge to make the depth cutline around the end of the stock.* **Step 3:** *Square down from the shoulder cutline to the depth cutline.*

Here I am simultaneously laying out four table legs for mortise holes from a story pole. To ensure accuracy, I clamp the legs together while holding a square across the ends.

I use a double-beamed mortise gauge, set to the width of the chisel that will help clean out the mortise, to mark both sides of the hole.

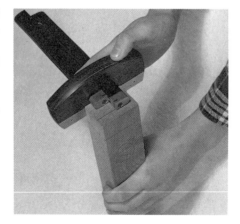

With the mortise gauge still set to the width of the mortise, I am marking the cutline of the tenon around the end of a piece of stock. Shoulder lines on the face of the stock indicate the extent of the cutlines.

tiple passes with the gauge instead of one heavy one. It is optional whether the stock is final cut to length at this point.

Finally, square down from the shoulder cutline to the centerline just created by the marking gauge. Fix the knife blade in the shoulder cut, slide the square to it, and run the blade down to the gauge line. Be sure to mark all the waste areas of the joint with an X.

Laying out mortise-and-tenon joints

When designing a mortise-and-tenon joint, plan to make the tenon's thickness about ⅓ to ½ the thickness of the stock in which the tenon will be cut. To ease the cutting process, lay out the width of the tenon to equal the width of the chisel you'll use to clean out the mortise.

Because the removal of the waste portions of the tenon would eliminate the overall length mark, cut this component to its final length prior to laying out the joint. Do not, however, cut the mortised component to length. If the mortise is near the end of the piece, the extra waste keeps the piece from splitting during waste removal.

Begin layout with the mortise. If there are identical mortises to be made in a series of identical components, clamp them together for marking. From these marks I will square across all four legs with a combination square. Note in the photo that I have used a square to ensure that the ends of the legs are flush. In the photo beneath, I am marking the width of the mortise with a mortise gauge. I set the pair of marking blades directly to the width of the chisel I am using, and then set the gauge's head to center the lines on the stock. Note that I'm running the head of the gauge against the side of the stock marked with the part symbol (which also indicates the outside face).

If the tenoned stock is the same thickness as the mortised stock, there is no need to change the head setting of the mortise gauge to mark the tenon. After marking the shoulder of the tenon joint with a knife and combination square, simply run the gauge around the end of the stock. Again, be sure that the head of the gauge is run to the side of the stock carrying the part symbol. This maintains the same reference point (the outside face) for both mortise and tenon layout lines, ensuring a flush surface when the joints are cut and fitted together. To lay out the length of the tenon, use the same marks on the story pole that laid out the length of the mortise hole.

Laying out a dovetail joint

Where would a book on layout procedures be without a section on laying out the most attractive, popular, and, for some, the most perplexing, joint of all: the dovetail? Probably not on your bookshelf unless you intend to do dovetail joints only with a machine. (If that's the case, don't read this section of the book, read the manual that came with the machine.)

Before going into laying out hand-cut dovetails, I should explain that the following procedures are for through-dovetails of uniform size spaced evenly across the width of a board. There are many other types of dovetail joints, such as blind (hidden), half-blind (showing on the side only) and mitered. Any one of these types may or may not have equally sized and spaced tails. (Variable sizing of dovetails is, by the way, something you cannot do with most dovetail cutting machines.) Much of the basic layout procedure is the same, however, for all types of dovetail joints.

When initially designing this joint for a particular application, keep these fundamental attributes of the dovetail joint in mind:

■ The tail of a dovetail joint acts as a stop wedge. It can be pulled apart from the side but not from the front. For this reason, lay out the tails on the side of the structure to which tension will be applied. This is, for example, why tails appear on the sides, rather than the fronts, of drawer boxes.

■ Generally speaking, the more tails, the greater the strength of the joint.

■ Don't design so many tails that the pins must be made less than ⅓ the size of the tails. Half the size is standard.

■ The angle of the dovetail should be between 8° to 12°. The stronger the wood, the greater (and prettier) you can make the angle. To keep the tails from becoming too fragile at their base, soft woods like pine must have lower tail angles.

While I acknowledge this may not hold for all woodworkers, the layout of a dovetail joint usually begins with the layout of the pins: First decide how many tails you wish the joint to have, and then divide the

Stress on a dovetailed drawer box. *Dovetails wedge tight as a drawer is pulled open.*

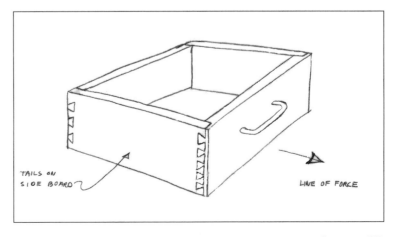

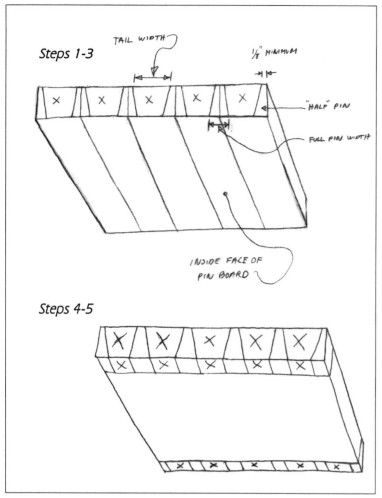

Steps 1-3

TAIL WIDTH

⅛" MINIMUM

"HALF" PIN

FULL PIN WIDTH

INSIDE FACE OF
PIN BOARD

Steps 4-5

Laying out the pins of a dovetail joint. Step 1: *Divide the board into the number of spaces equal to the desired number of tails.* **Step 2:** *Lay out "half" pins at either end of the board with a dovetail gauge angle.* **Step 3:** *Draw full pins on the ends of the boards. Center them on the division lines and make them ⅓ to ½ the size of the tails (represented by the Xed area.)* **Step 4:** *Run the shoulderline (at the thickness of the tail stock).* **Step 5:** *Square the pin lines down to the shoulderline. Mark the waste area and erase the divider lines.*

in the half-pins at either edge of the board. These pins do not actually have to be ½ the full size of the pins. They should, however, be at least ⅛" thick at their narrowest point. Draw the pin angle with a knife set against a bevel gauge locked down to the desired angle. If you don't mind being permanently committed to a specific angle, you can use a commercially made dovetail marker gauge. Otherwise, make a gauge at any angle you desire from a scrap of metal and a hardwood block, as shown in the drawing.

Now roughly sketch in the tails between the division lines to give you an idea of how they will look. Orient the narrow side of the tails toward the inside face of the pin board. Size the tails so that the pins centered on the division lines come out ½ to ⅓ the size of the tails. Draw in the pins with the gauge and a knife, centering them on the division lines. To prevent any confusion, shade in or make an *X* between the pins.

Set a marking gauge to the thickness of the stock in which the tails will be made. (Don't measure. Instead, hold the gauge to a sample of the stock.) Run the head of the gauge against the end of the board (double-check to be sure it's square cut), making a line around the circumference of the board. Square down from the pin lines to this shoulder line on both the inside and outside faces of the board. Be sure to mark the waste areas between the pins on the end and on both faces of the board.

That waste area between the pins looks suspiciously like the tails of a dovetail joint. Not too surprising: That's exactly what they repre-

board on which the pins will be laid out into this number of sections with the angled rule method shown earlier in this chapter. The board should already be square cut to length. Draw these division marks across the end grain of the board.

These division lines represent the centers of the pins. Now draw

sent. Using a sharp pencil or marking knife, transfer this "waste" area to the board on which the tails are to be cut by holding the boards end to end, outside faces facing out. Then use a small try square, or the square portion of your handmade dovetail marker, to square the marks across the end of the board.

Now set the marking gauge to the thickness of the board laid out for pins (it may or may not be the same as the tail's board), and run the shoulder line all the way around. Use the bevel gauge or dovetail gauge to draw the angled tail cutlines back from the end of the board to the shoulder on either side of the board. Shade or X in the areas between the tails. The pins and tails are now laid out for cutting.

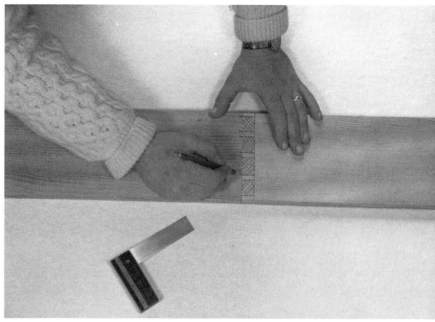

Holding the stock to receive tails against the end of the pin board is a quick and error free way to transfer the layout. The tails are marked from the waste area between the pins.

Shop-made dovetail marking gauge. *Make the body of the gauge from stable hardwood. Joint the sides straight and perpendicular to the top surface.*

Chapter 6
Cutting to the Lines

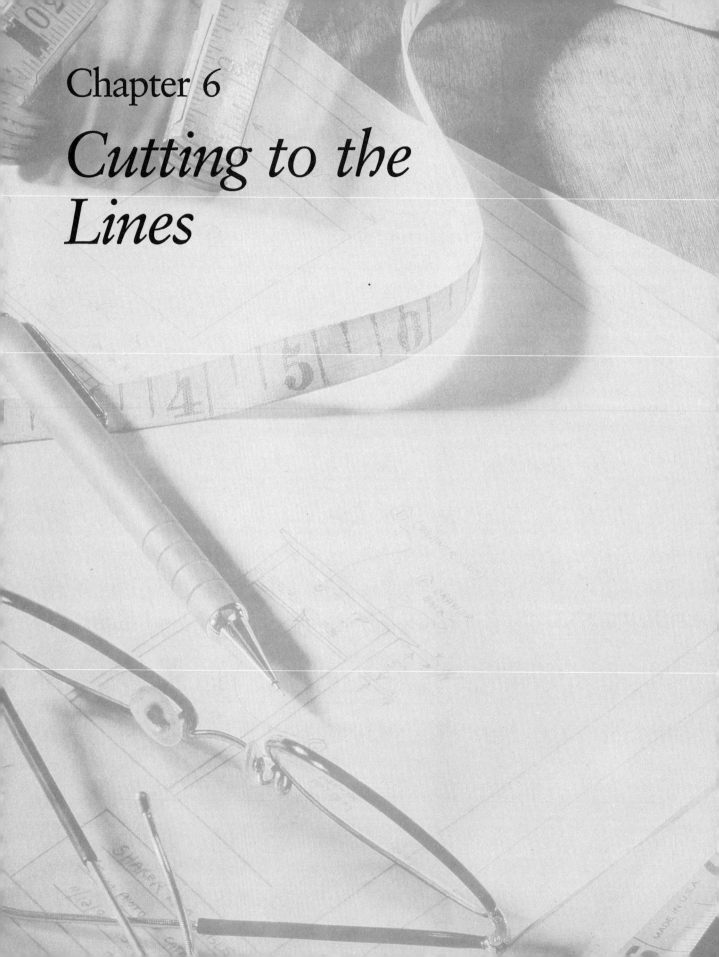

You've probably heard about the old carpenter who complained: "I cut it twice and it's still too short!" Obviously he could benefit by reading the first five chapters in this book about measuring right the first time. At the very least, he would get the platitude right, if not the cut.

"Measure twice, cut once." It means paying close attention to your working drawings to get the proportions right. It means laying out the components to full scale to check their accuracy and to provide a way to transfer the dimensions directly onto story poles. And, finally, it means carefully aligning and securing the poles to the stock to get down the cutlines. Having done all this, all that is left to do is to make the cuts. There may still, however, be one thing left to complain about: the quality of the cut itself.

For no matter how good the layout, the success of the end result depends on how well the cuts are made. Whether by hand or machine, each cut must precisely follow the lines that you have made for it. If the cuts are to be repeated in identical components, the jigs and stops controlling the cuts must be accurate and they must stay that way. In this chapter I will show you how to set up and use tools to make accurate cuts, and how to test the components prior to final assembly.

Crosscutting Procedures

Crosscutting is perhaps the most common woodworking operation. Every component must be crosscut to its final length, and nearly every

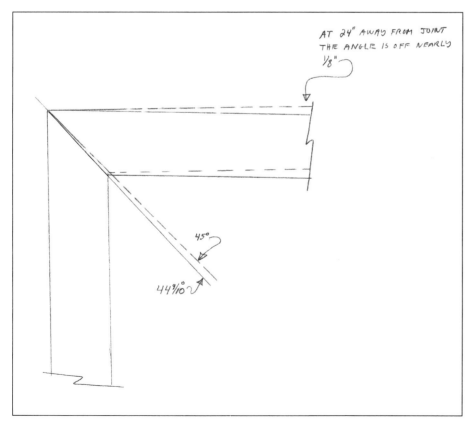

AT 24" AWAY FROM JOINT
THE ANGLE IS OFF NEARLY
1/8"

45°

44 9/10°

Effect of a miscut miter joint. *As an example, if a 45° miter cut is off by only 1/5°, the total error is 1/10°. This throws off the angle of assembly by almost 1/64" for every 3" of run.*

this just as quickly.)

To reduce error, and to make efficient use of your time, group all components that require similar, if not identical, cuts. For example, gather the components that need to be square crosscut to length, even if they are unrelated within the structure. After crosscutting, you can re-collate the pieces into other process-related groupings. This is also a good time to consider re-marking any smudged or faded part or orientation symbols.

Crosscutting With Hand Tools

The saw I most commonly use for crosscutting solid stock to length is a 10-point, 24″-long panel saw. I'll use a rougher, but faster cutting, 8-point saw if the cut does not have to be particularly clean. When cutting smaller stock to length, I like to use my Japanese Ryoba combination saw. It is very fast, yet it leaves a clean cut. The opposite side of the blade is fixed with rip teeth—handy if I'm cutting notches or other cuts that run parallel to the grain. Because the Ryoba cuts on the pull stroke (just the opposite of the saws of Europe and America), it takes some getting used to.

For the fine crosscutting of joint lines, or cutting very small stock to length, I use one of my backsaws. Because of their small teeth, these saws cut cleanly but comparatively slowly. The stiffener running along the top of a backsaw's blade ensures a very straight cut.

To ensure your handsaws cut smoothly, always keep the blade clean and free of rust. I find a coat of paraffin to be the most durable and effective barrier to rust, while

Depending on the size and number of teeth, the performance of a crosscut saw ranges from that of the swift, though coarse cutting, 8 teeth-per-inch panel saw to that of the slow, but fine cutting dovetail saw. From left to right, an 8 teeth-per-inch panel, a 12 teeth-per-inch panel, a Japanese Ryoba combination saw, a backsaw and a Japanese dovetail saw.

joint contains at least one cut across the wood grain. Because even a minute error in the angle of the cut can result in major problems with the overall dimensions and shape of a structure, it's critical that your crosscuts be accurate.

For power tools to cut well, you must carefully set them up so that they cut true to their own reference surfaces. For example, adjust a circular saw's base plate to rest at precisely 90° to the blade when it's secured down to its stop. And, whenever possible, run power tools against guides and shop-made jigs.

Hand tools, by contrast, depend entirely on you for accuracy. A well-sharpened handsaw, for instance, goes only where your hand tells it to go. But with a little practice (maybe a little more than a little) hand tools can produce as clean and accurate a joint line as any machine. (And in some instances, they can do

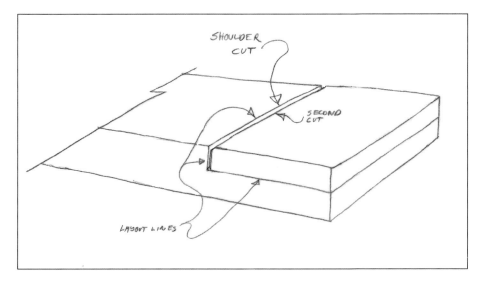

SHOULDER CUT

SECOND CUT

LAYOUT LINES

Creating a cutting shoulder. *Create a cutting shoulder at the crosscut layout lines by first cutting straight into the wood with a sharp knife. Make the cutting shoulder by angling a second cut in toward the first — the resulting groove need only be about ⅛″ deep.*

also providing the greatest degree of cutting lubrication. Avoid using a saw with a kinked blade; you'll never get it to cut a straight line. Finally, to extend the life of the teeth, avoid cutting through glue lines or painted surfaces. I reserve an old saw for those occasions when there is no choice.

If you marked the cutlines with a knife, you have already severed the wood fibers below the surface of the board. If, on the waste side of the line, you make a second knife cut at a 45° angle toward the layout line, you will create a shoulder on which to hold the saw blade. This makes it easier to control the line of the cut. Make this shoulder not only across, but also down the sides of the board along the layout line.

To start the cut, set the saw blade in the layout groove at the corner of the wood facing away from you and pull back on the saw with a series of small strokes. (If using the Japanese Ryoba, lightly push, instead of pull, the saw.) Because the teeth are designed to cut in the opposite direction, the saw

will be unaggressive, making only a small kerf. Be sure you have set the saw on the waste side of the layout line. Use the knuckle of your thumb on your free hand as a temporary guide to support the saw vertically in the cut. *Safety note:* Be sure only

Get a crosscut off to a good start by using your thumb knuckle to guide the blade to the mark.

I guide a backsaw along a cut by extending my first finger alongside the saw. This gives the blade directional support and gives my hand a better sense of where the saw is cutting.

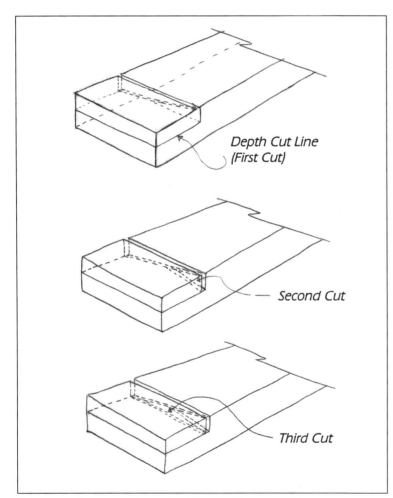

Depth Cut Line
(First Cut)

Second Cut

Third Cut

Using a backsaw to make a shoulder cut. First cut: *Make the first cut across the top and down to the depth cutline on the far edge.* **Second cut:** *Keep the blade in the top cut as you bring the side cut on the facing edge to the depth cutline.* **Third cut:** *Hold the saw parallel to the top surface and cut until the blade touches the cutlines on both edges.*

to pull the saw while your thumb is in this position—move it away before sawing aggressively.

Once the cut is about ¼" deep, begin sawing in earnest. Holding the panel saw at about a 45° angle to the face of the wood, take long smooth strokes, exerting force only on the down stroke. The sharper the saw, the less elbow grease will be required.

To keep the saw cutting parallel to the layout lines on the edges of the board, hold a square (an old 8" to 10" 45° to 45° plastic drafting template is ideal for this purpose) to the side of the saw blade as you cut. If the edge line is at an angle, set a bevel gauge to this angle and hold that to the blade as a reference. Support the offcut so that its weight doesn't split it away from the stock near the end of the cut.

Creating a shoulder cut with a backsaw or dovetail saw requires a somewhat different technique. First, check your grip: To maintain fine control of the saw, position your index finger alongside the saw. With straight handled dovetail saws, exert a slight, but steady, counterclockwise rotation in your wrist to maintain the cut square to the surface. This counteracts the natural tendency of your hand to hold the saw at an angle.

Begin the cut in the same way as you did for a panel saw, and then proceed with the power strokes. This time, however, lower the angle of the blade so that the cut continues all the way across the board while the far end of the blade still emerges from the edge cut. For the second cut, use the kerf created by the first cut to guide the saw blade down the layout line on the edge facing you. Make the last cut by lifting up the saw to cut parallel with the surface down to the bottom of the cuts on either edge.

Fixtures to aid hand-crosscutting

When making a shoulder cut with a backsaw, two fixtures are quite useful. The first, a bench hook, gives you a place to firmly hold the stock in place while cutting. Toggle clamps can be added if you wish, and the hook itself can be temporarily screwed down to the workbench.

The second fixture is a depth stop clamped to the blade of the saw. Made from a straight-edged

length of wood set to the depth of the cut (measured up from the edge of the blade), this fixture is invaluable when making long cuts where you can't see how deep the saw is cutting along any edge.

The ubiquitous miter box is probably the most famous hand-crosscutting fixture of all. Although a crude one can be made for the backsaw from three slabs of wood, with just a little use the guide kerfs soon widen, making the fixture intolerably inaccurate. Instead, I use an ancient 1920s-era Sears steel-

A stick clamped to the side of a backsaw blade provides a depth stop—especially useful when the position of the blade can't be judged against a depth mark on the stock's edge. Here I am cutting the shoulder of a rabbet joint.

Bench hook. Glue and screw boards to a plywood table.

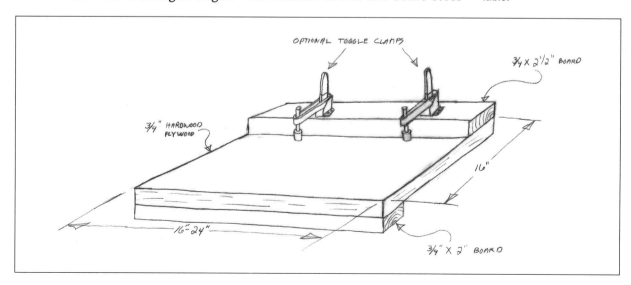

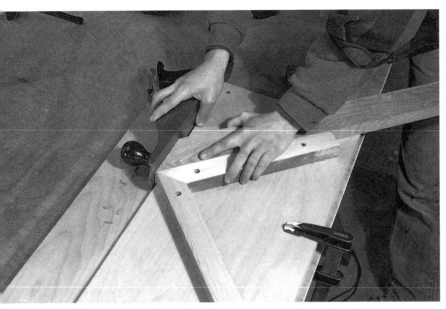

When trimming the mitered end of a piece of wood to fit, I use a sharp plane and a shop-made shooting board to hold the stock. This combination allows me to remove fine shavings at a controlled angle.

Three miterboxes: my ancient Sears hand-powered miter box flanked by a 10" power chop saw to the left and an 8½" sliding compound miter saw to the right. The cut produced by each of these miter boxes is clean and accurate. While the powered boxes have the advantage of speed and the ability to trim off fine shavings, the hand-powered box is joyfully quiet to use.

framed miter box. It is extremely accurate, and a joy to use. The one drawback of this miter box, common to all hand-powered boxes, is that it needs at least a saw blade's width of wood to cut on. This means you cannot use it (as you can a power miter box) to skim off fractions of an inch for final trimming to the line.

So what did woodworkers do before power miter boxes you might ask? They used shooting boards and planes to trim the cuts to their final fits. A sharp plane can remove shavings as small as two-thousandths of an inch, well within the tolerances of most woodworking projects I've been involved with.

In the photograph, I am fine-trimming a miter cut with a jack plane and a 45° shooting board. I first cut the piece on the miter box to length on the waste side of the layout line, being careful to leave the line itself. Then, with the plane's blade honed sharp and squared to the side of the plane body (I check it with a combination square and then run the plane by a piece of scrap to be sure), I plane the end of the stock to the layout line. (I have to be careful to not plane against the jig itself, or I might eventually remove enough wood to throw off the angle.) Because the angled stop was set at exactly 45° to the edge of the shooting board, the plane cuts a perfect 45° miter. You can, of course, set up shooting boards to hold the stock at any angle desired, including 90° square cuts.

Crosscutting With Portable Power Tools

I'll have to admit that my old Sears miter box does not see the use it

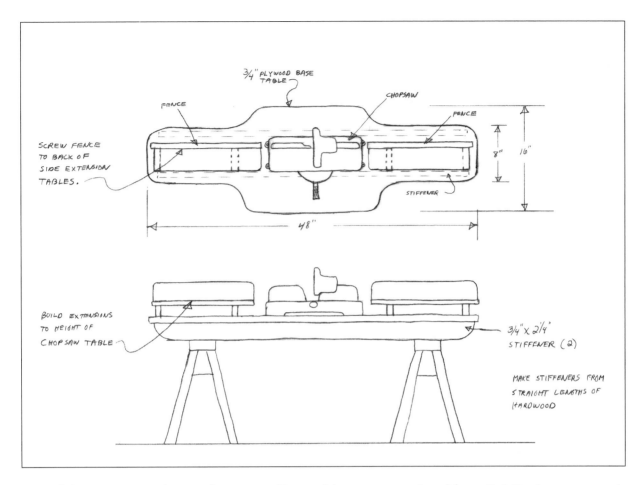

3/4" PLYWOOD BASE TABLE

FENCE

CHOPSAW

FENCE

SCREW FENCE TO BACK OF SIDE EXTENSION TABLES.

STIFFENER

8" 16"

48"

BUILD EXTENSIONS TO HEIGHT OF CHOPSAW TABLE

3/4" X 2 1/4" STIFFENER (2)

MAKE STIFFENERS FROM STRAIGHT LENGTHS OF HARDWOOD

Portable chop saw support.

once did. For crosscutting stock up to about 4½″ wide, I now almost exclusively use a 10″ power miter saw. I also own an 8½″ slide compound saw for cutting compound miter angles in stock up to 12″ wide. If time is of the essence, there is no substitute for this last tool for making complex crosscuts.

To help these miter boxes work to peak efficiency, set up tables on either side to support the stock. Use a long straightedge to be sure the supports are level with the tool's table surface. Because I move my chop saw around the shop, and sometimes to job sites as well, I made a portable support table for my chop saw that I can lay across a pair of sawhorses.

For making crosscuts in wider boards and sheet stock, I usually use a 7″ circular saw. (On thin sheet stock — ¼″ or less — I find that a specialized cordless panel circular saw is much easier to handle.) Before using the circular saw, I make sure that its base plate, when fixed against its stop, is square to the blade. First I visually orient the plate to the blade using a small try square as a guide, adjusting the stop as necessary. Then I make a test cut through a 1½″ scrap of wood and test the cut against the square. If the cut is off, I adjust the stop and try again.

I don't bother to confirm the accuracy of the depth gauge of the circular saw because I always make test cuts to determine the blade depth.

Holding a protractor guide securely to the board ensures that I make a straight crosscut with my power saw. The protractor can be set to guide the saw at any angle across the board.

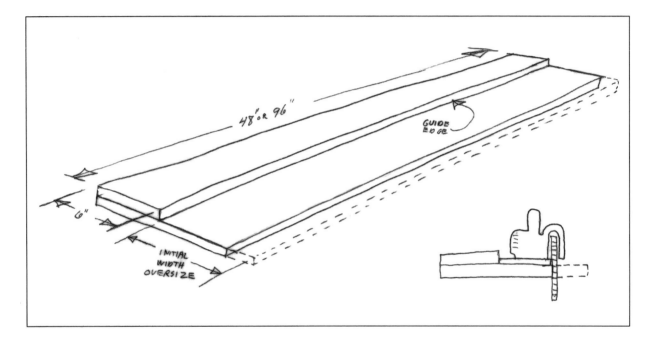

48″ OR 96″

GUIDE EDGE

6″

INITIAL WIDTH OVERSIZE

Panel cutting saw guide. Make the guide from ½″ hardwood plywood. Be sure the guide edge is perfectly straight. Cut the guide to width by running a saw along the guide edge.

Even if the gauge was accurate, I find that I often don't know the measurement in numbers anyway. To reduce errors, I always try to set cutlines to actual dimensions, such as the lines on a story pole or to the stem of a depth gauge.

Guides and fixtures for controlling the angle of the crosscut

I learned long ago that I was incapable of making a perfectly straight cut across a wide board or sheet without using some kind of fixture or guide. When crosscutting boards with a circular saw, I nearly always use a protractor tool to guide the base of the saw. On panel stock, I make up a full-length guide. Note that the saw itself is used to cut the guide's index edge to width from the stop. Because of this, always use the same saw, and preferably the same blade, with this particular guide. This helps maintain the accuracy of the index

Because a sheet of plywood's factory edge is not always straight or perpendicular to the side, I use a panel square and router to true the edge. The panel square acts as a template for an overcutter bearing router bit.

edge when setting it to the cut lines.

To use the guide to make a long cut across a piece of sheet stock, set the guide's index edge directly on the layout marks made on opposite edges of the sheet and clamp the fixture securely to the stock. When running the circular saw, be sure to keep the base plate firmly and consistently tight against the stop.

Squaring up a sheet stock panel's factory edge

In addition to laying out long square cuts, I use a shop-made panel square as a template for guiding a router along the end of a piece of sheeting to true the factory edge. Because many of the layout measurements are referenced to this edge, they can only be as precise as the edge itself. This technique assures that this edge is straight and square to the long side of the sheet.

To true the factory edge, clamp the panel square across the sheet near the end, being sure the side leg is firmly against the long edge of the sheet. Clear any splinters or staples that might hold it away, throwing the square off. Leave 1/16" of the sheet protruding past the square.

Now install a 1/2" or 5/8" straight-fluted router bit with a pilot bearing mounted over the cutters (see Appendix A for sources) into the router and run the router along the leg of the panel square. Be sure to set the depth of cut so that the pilot bearing runs only against the edge of the square—it shouldn't touch the edge of the sheet. The resulting cut will be an exact replica of the template: straight and square.

Crosscutting With Stationary Tools

Ever since I've been doing woodworking, I've heard the argument rage among woodworkers about which tool is the most versatile and worthwhile to own: the table saw or the radial arm saw. Of course, it depends on the type of woodworking they're talking about. A cabinetmaker who deals primarily with

Jigs designed to slide in the miter grooves of a table saw will not perform well unless the saw's blade is parallel to these grooves. I test the parallelism of the table saw blade to the saw table's miter grooves with a combination square. The blade of the square should just touch a marked saw tooth at both the back, and then toward the front, of the machine.

Slide crosscut box for the tablesaw. Make the front and back fences from straight lengths of wood 1¼" thick by 2½" high.

sheet stock has little use for a radial arm saw with its limited crosscutting width capacity, while a furniture-maker can get away without the larger capacity of a table saw. I solved the argument in my own shop by owning both.

I use the radial arm saw almost exclusively for crosscutting stock up to about 16" in width. When dealing with long and heavy boards, I find it easier and much more efficient to use than the table saw for this purpose. When ripping stock to width, however, I use the table saw. I know you can rip with the radial arm saw, but only a die-hard R.A.S.F. (Radial Arm Saw Freak) would tell you it's easy and fun to do.

Crosscutting on the table saw

The table saw is, however, eminently well suited to crosscutting wide sheet stock components or assemblies such as cabinet doors. As long as their edges are square to one another, you can set the rip fence of the saw to the measurement and index an edge of the component to

it. For an accurate, straight cut, the fence must be set parallel to the blade. To do this, see the section later in this chapter.

For safety's sake, I never crosscut a component less than 16" in width with the rip fence acting as the only guide. There is the chance that narrower stock will shift, jam against the blade, and kick back with tremendous force. When I do crosscut narrow stock on the table saw, I use one of several versions of a shop-made sliding crosscut box. (I rarely use the miter gauge that came with the saw as a guide for crosscutting: The single guide bar of these gauges allows too much play.) Note the long fence along the front edge of the box. I install a right-to-left reading tape and a sliding stop along the fence to the left of the blade, which allows me to quickly set dimensioned crosscuts without having to measure each cut separately with a handheld rule.

Before beginning construction of the crosscut box, make sure that the blade of the saw is parallel to the

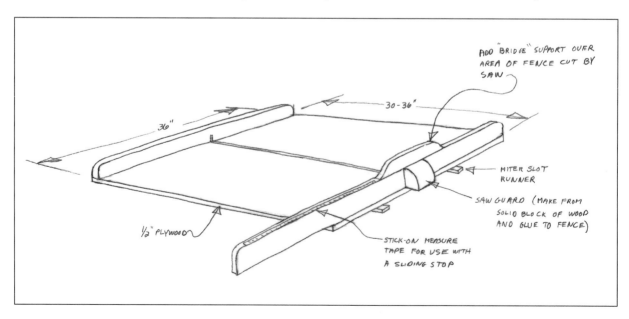

ADD "BRIDGE" SUPPORT OVER AREA OF FENCE CUT BY SAW

30-36"

36"

MITER SLOT RUNNER

SAW GUARD (MAKE FROM SOLID BLOCK OF WOOD AND GLUE TO FENCE)

½" PLYWOOD

STICK-ON MEASURE TAPE FOR USE WITH A SLIDING STOP

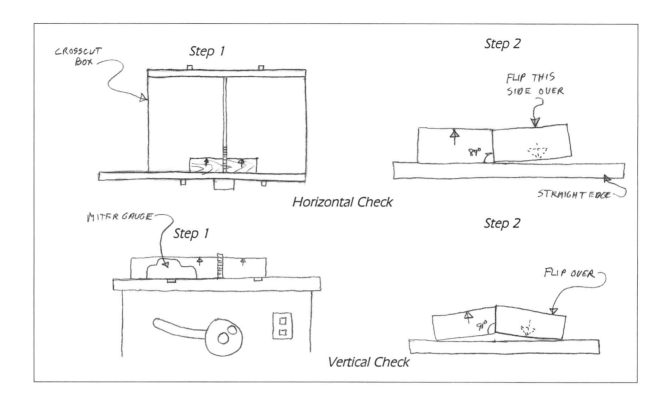

Horizontal Check

Step 1 — CROSSCUT BOX

Step 2 — FLIP THIS SIDE OVER — 87° — STRAIGHT EDGE

Vertical Check

Step 1 — MITER GAUGE

Step 2 — FLIP OVER — 91°

machined table grooves (in which the guides of the box will ride). You can do this quickly with your combination square: First, unplug the machine and raise the blade as high as it will go. Find a tooth even with the surface of the table toward the back of the saw and mark it with a pen or piece of masking tape. Set the head of the square against a table groove and run out the square's blade until it just touches the marked tooth. Now rotate the blade so the marked tooth is even with the table at the front of the machine. Slide the square along the groove and check to see if the blade again just touches the tooth. If it does, the sawblade is parallel to the grooves. If it doesn't, loosen the bolts holding the table to the base of the machine and adjust it. (Use a rubber mallet to persuade the table to move in small increments.)

To make the crosscut box, first cut two guides out of hardwood (the self-lubricating, durable nature of teak or lignum vitae make them ideal choices) and fit them to the table grooves so they slide freely, but without play. Then cut the box's platform to size from hardwood plywood and set it over the installed guides. Flush the edge of the platform with the face edge of the saw's table. (At this point, the table saw's blade should be all the way down, and the machine unplugged.) After screwing through the platform into the guides, slide the table back and forth to test the glide.

Because the screwing operation shifts things a bit, the platform will not likely slide very easily. To loosen it up, run a cabinet scraper along the edges of the guides. But not everywhere. Find the areas of the guides that are binding by paint-

Test to check the horizontal squareness of the cut. Step 1: *Crosscut a ¾″ × 6″ test board. (The board must have parallel edges.)* **Step 2:** *Hold the test pieces to a straightedge as shown. If the crosscut is any angle other than 90°, a gap will appear at the end or middle.*

Test to check the vertical squareness of the cut. Step 1: *Stand a ¾″ × 3″ test board on edge and run it through the blade.* **Step 2:** *Hold pieces to a straightedge and check for a gap.*

This sliding miter box produces 45° crosscuts across boards up to about 6" wide. The boards can be set in the box and mitered from either the right or the left—this means that the outside (the good face) of the stock always faces up.

ing machinist's bluing (see Appendix A) along the edges of the machined grooves and then sliding the platform back and forth. The bluing comes off on the edges of the guides on the high spots. A few light passes with the cabinet scraper at these spots are usually enough to allow the platform to slide freely. Don't overdo it or you'll introduce play in the travel of the box.

With the platform set in place and held down with clamps, turn on the saw and raise the blade through the plywood. Stop the machine and unclamp the platform. Now turn it back on and slowly run the platform forward, stopping when the cut is about 2" away from the facing edge. Lower the blade fully and hold a framing square along the edge of the cut. Set the fence in position and align it to the square, temporarily screwing either end to the platform.

To check if the fence is perfectly perpendicular to the blade, make a test cut on a 6"-wide scrap of wood whose edges are parallel and straight. Crosscut the scrap in half and then flip over one of the pieces and rejoin them together. If the cut is a perfect 90°, no gap will appear when you hold them to a straight-

Multi-angle sliding miter box. *Make the front and back fences from 1¼" × 2" stock. Make a semicircular slot for the carriage bolt. Rout the underside so the bolt head is flush to the plywood.*

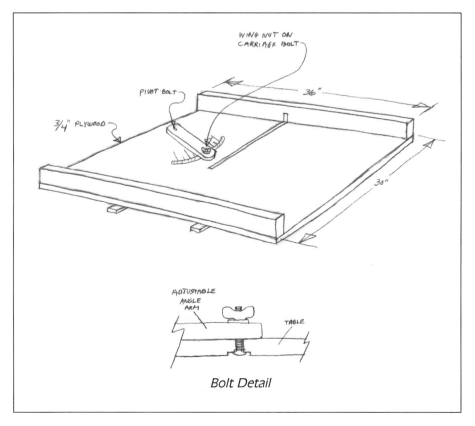

Bolt Detail

edge. Adjust the fence until the test cuts are gap-free, and then screw the fence permanently to the platform. Install another fence at the far end of the platform to act as a stiffener— it doesn't have to be square to the blade.

This is also a good time to check that the table saw's carriage stop is set so the blade cuts a perfect 90° vertical to the table (and thus the sliding box platform). Use the same test described previously, this time checking to see that the cut is square to the face of the stock. Consult the saw's manual for instructions on how to adjust the stop.

I also use two other types of sliding crosscut boxes on the table saw. One is used exclusively for cutting 45° miter angles while the other is adjustable, allowing me to make crosscuts at a variety of angles. To build these boxes, follow the same procedure just described for making the 90° crosscut box.

Setting depth of cut

To ensure accuracy, always set the depth of cut by cutting test pieces and checking these against actual dimensions, such as story pole layout marks, sizes of components or a rule, if the former two references aren't available.

To set the depth of a cut to the exact midpoint of a thickness of stock (for example, when crosscutting shoulder and waste cuts for a half-lap joint), do not measure. Instead, make a series of cuts in a test piece the same thickness as the stock. Do not rush the test—bring the blade up slowly until only a whisper of wood remains between the top and bottom cuts.

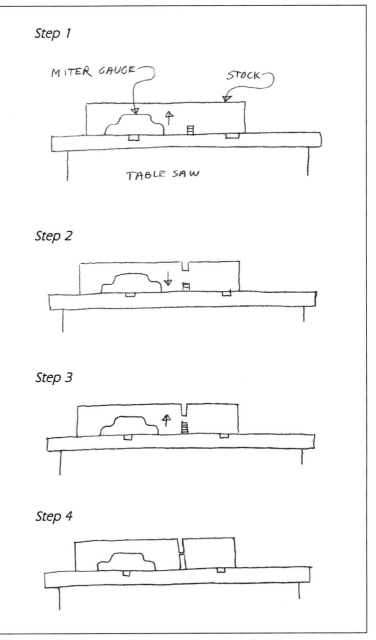

Setting the blade height to midpoint of the stock. Step 1: Set the blade height to less than half the thickness of the stock and make a crosscut. Step 2: Flip the stock over and cut under the first crosscut. Step 3: Raise the blade slightly and make another pass. Flip the board over and cut. Step 4: Continue the process until only a paper-thin piece of wood remains between the cuts.

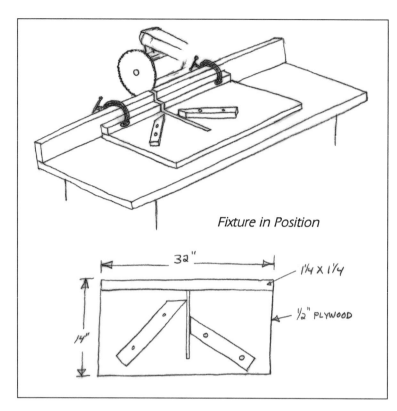

Fixture in Position

32"

1¼ × 1¼

½" PLYWOOD

14"

Miter box fixture for a radial arm saw. *Make fences from ¾" × 2" straight-edged stock. Set at 45° to the cutline.*

Crosscutting with a radial arm saw

To get the most out of a radial arm saw, take the time to set up the machine according to the manufacturer's directions. Additional, and probably clearer, information can usually be found in books. Use the same tests described previously for

When a board is ripped, the release of internal stresses often closes the kerf around the rip saw. To prevent this, I place a cedar shim in the kerf just ahead of the blade to keep it open. Also note the high angle at which I am holding the saw—rip teeth cut more efficiently at a high angle of attack.

determining the accuracy of the crosscuts across and through the depth of the stock.

I find that my radial arm saw stays in alignment much longer if I use it only for crosscutting. This is another reason why I prefer to use the table saw for ripping. I generally try to avoid changing the crosscut angle setting from 90°, using another shop-made jig when I want to cut miter joints on molding stock. Note that the fences are offset from one another to allow the rough cut stock to be aligned to their cut marks.

Ripping Procedures

In my experience, ripping stock to width is not as much fun as crosscutting. Perhaps those days that found me hand-ripping long pine floor boards with a less-than-sharp rip saw have colored my view of this process. Or perhaps it's my nose still twitching at the thought of all that sawdust hurtling back at me as I ran acrid oak stock through the table saw (in those less enlightened days before my dust collection system was in operation). With the right tools and techniques, however, the process of ripping boards need not be festooned with such anxiety-ridden memories.

Using Hand Tools to Rip Stock to Width

For hand-ripping stock to width, I, along with many other woodworkers, choose a five to seven teeth-per-inch panel-type rip saw. For smaller rip cuts, I often use the rip-toothed side of my Japanese Ryoba saw. When I want to make refined cuts (such as tenons and dovetails), I use a backsaw with teeth resharpened for ripping. Because each tooth must act as a chisel when cutting with the grain of the wood, as opposed to a shearing knife when crosscutting, the saw chops, instead of slices, its way through the wood. And because chopping encounters much more resistance than slicing, rip cuts generally go slower than crosscuts, and hardly go at all if the teeth are not well sharpened.

Start a rip cut in a similar way to starting a crosscut: Position the blade on the waste side of the mark, supporting it vertically with the thumb knuckle. Repeatedly pull back on the saw to start a shallow cut, and then, very gently at first, begin the power strokes in the opposite direction. Give yourself a bit more of a starting cut when ripping with the coarser teeth of a rip saw.

Make the power strokes at a higher angle than you used in crosscutting: about 60° to the surface. Insert a cedar shim to keep the kerf from closing in behind the cut. Finally, be sure to support the offcut so that it doesn't pull away near the end of the cut, sending a split into the good side of the board.

Ripping With Portable Power Tools

For ripping solid wood to width, I use a 7″ to 10″ circular saw. As with the handsaw, the sharper the blade, the faster the tool cuts. For the most part, a carbide-tipped combination blade works well enough for rip cutting, though a blade sharpened exclusively for ripping will cut faster and will not dull as quickly. A dedicated rip blade will generally, however, produce a somewhat wider kerf—account for this when laying out the components on the stock.

If the wood binds against a table saw's blade when being ripped, the board may be flung across the room. I prevent this from happening by installing a short auxiliary fence. Because the fence ends at the back of the blade, it allows a reactive piece of wood to freely move away from the blade.

During layout, also allow plenty of extra width in the rough cut to joint the ripped boards straight. With most woods, ⅛″ extra is sufficient. If you make the first rip cut and see that this stock is going to bend considerably (and the components are long lengths), you may need to allow up to a ¼″ waste margin. At this point you might be better off substituting a board that's not so reactive, and using the ripped board for short components.

Most circular saws are designed to accept some kind of rip guide. Of course, the guidance they give the blade is only as good as the reference edge they are asked to run against. When ripping stock with a circular saw and guide, always joint the reference edge. As in hand-ripping, be prepared to wedge the cut open behind the saw, and always support the offcut.

Ripping on the Table Saw

The easiest, most efficient way I know of to rip boards to width is on

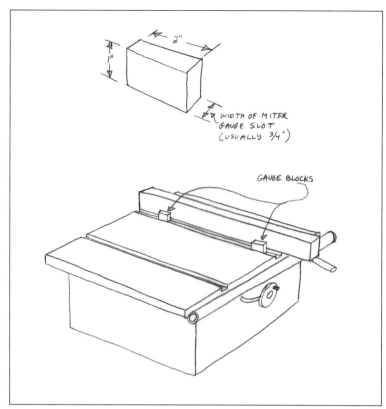

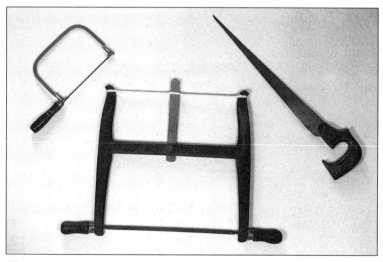

Alignment of a table saw fence to gauge blocks. *Make the blocks from hardwood.*

These hand tools designed for cutting curves share several traits: The blades are narrow to allow them to follow a curve without the back of the blade binding, and the teeth are sharpened for ripping, allowing them to cut faster in most cutting situations. In the center is a bow-type scroll saw. To the left is a coping saw, and to the right a compass saw.

a table saw. Ripping is what a table saw does best. With a sharp, thin kerf, aggressive rip blade (24 teeth-per-inch is a good choice), stock less than 1″ in thickness usually runs through the blade with almost no effort on the part of the saw operator.

To prevent stock from binding behind the blade, always use a splitter in line with and behind the blade (this accessory usually comes with the saw). If the stock is really squirrelly, immediately curling away from the cut as it leaves the blade, stop cutting and install an auxiliary fence whose length ends at the far end of the blade.

Binding can also occur, even when ripping a stable board, if the fence is not set parallel to the blade. Adjust the fence so that when you lock it down, it seats itself properly. If you took the time to orient the blade parallel to the machined grooves, you can align the fence to gauge blocks set into one of these miter slots. Follow the manufacturer's instructions for adjusting the angle of the fence relative to its carriage along the front rail.

Cutting to Curves

I find ripping boards to length with a handsaw to be a lot of fun. I also find climbing on a Stairmaster and eating raw garlic to be fun. Sure I do—in reality, ripping is a drag. But cutting to curves is just the opposite. Either by hand or power, it always gives me a thrill to see sinuous, fair curves emerge from the path of a saw blade. Especially if I planned it that way.

Generally speaking, tools intended for cutting curves are very narrow-bladed saws set with rip teeth. This is true for each of the

hand tools: the coping saw; its larger cousin, the bow-framed scroll saw; and a thin-bladed variety of the panel saw, the compass saw. It's also true for jigsaws (sometimes also called "bayonet" or "saber" saws), and stationary band and scroll saws.

Cutting curves with hand saws

The coping saw is designed to make fine, tight-radius curves (down to a ⅛″ radius) in relatively thin (less than 1″) stock. I usually install an 18 teeth-per-inch blade with the teeth angled toward the handle. This means that the saw's power occurs on the pull, rather than the push stroke. I find this provides more support for the blade, resulting in less wander in the cut.

As the photo shows, I cut from below the board. This cutting action not only reduces tearout, it also pulls the stock to the support surface as I make the cut. I hold the stock against a V-cut board clamped to the workbench.

I use a compass saw to make larger radius curves in stock ¾″ or greater. Unless the saw is a Japanese model, the power comes on the push stroke. To avoid kinking the blade, I try to keep the blade sharp and to take only short power strokes, especially as the curve tightens. Unfortunately, you won't find a compass saw in my toolbox without a kinked blade.

Cutting curves with a jigsaw

The best jigsaws have variable speed controls and, more important, variable orbit reciprocal action. This action adds a forward element to the cutting action of the blade. The greater this movement, the more aggressive the cut. A jigsaw with these features, and fitted with a sharp blade, can quickly cut tight curves (down to about a ⅜″ radius) in hardwood. It is unnecessary to push a saw with these features, only to guide it. However, because the coarseness of the cut is directly proportional to the reciprocal action, I adjust my saw to the minimum reciprocal action necessary to get the blade through the cut without binding.

Jigsaw blades are designed to cut on the pull stroke. This cutting action pulls the stock to the base of the machine. While this greatly reduces vibration and extends the life of the blade, there is a drawback: The "fuzzy" side of the cut occurs at the top surface of the stock. If you are cutting thin veneers, or plywood with a fragile facing, this can cause severe tearout. To avoid disaster, either lay out and cut on the underside (the "bad side") of the stock, or make the layout lines with firm knife cuts. In the latter case, you must be very careful to cut only on the waste side of the line.

Cutting circles with a jigsaw

Because it can be cumbersome to cut large circles (a tabletop for example) with a band saw, I use a shop-made

I set the blade of the coping saw to cut on the down stroke, reducing the tearout on the laid-out side of the stock. I hold the handle of the saw below the work, and pull the blade down into the cut. Note the V-shaped block that supports the stock.

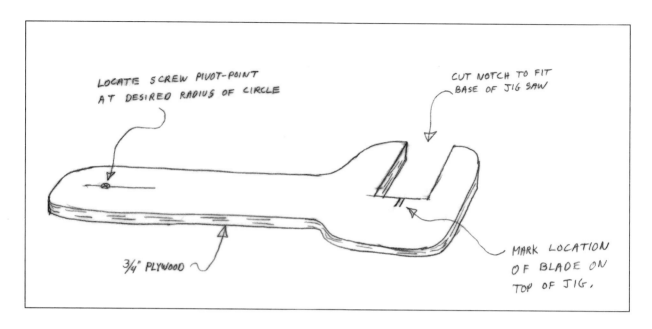

LOCATE SCREW PIVOT-POINT
AT DESIRED RADIUS OF CIRCLE

CUT NOTCH TO FIT
BASE OF JIG SAW

3/4" PLYWOOD

MARK LOCATION
OF BLADE ON
TOP OF JIG.

Circle cutting jig for the jig-saw.

fixture with a jigsaw to do the job. Working with a sharp blade and a steady motion, I find that this fixture guides the jigsaw to cut a smooth, uniform circle. Note the one drawback of this method: A screw hole must be made into the stock at the center point of the circle. If there is an underside to the component, mount the fixture on this side where the hole will not matter.

Cutting curves on a band saw

The premier tool for cutting curves is the band saw. Of course, there is also a large fan club for the scroll saw as well. But while the scroll saw's removable blade does allow it to cut interior openings, it cuts more slowly than the band saw, and with no tighter a radius. In my book, the band saw is the stationary machine for cutting curves.

For the best performance, you must tune up your band saw to reduce blade wobble. Follow the manufacturer's instructions to set wheel

alignment, blade tension, tracking and the angle stops on the table. Unless your manual tells you otherwise, set the guide blocks about 1/64" to the rear of the tooth gullets, and just touching the blade without dragging. Set the thrust bearings to within 1/64" of the back of the blade. To further reduce the tendency of the blade to wander in the cut, keep the upper guide assembly raised to just above (within 1/4") the thickness of the stock being cut.

As shown in the illustration, pick the width of the blade that will cut the minimum radius to be encountered in the curve. In general, I choose the widest blade I think I can get away with, as the wider the blade, the easier it is to maintain a smooth cut along a curve. The blade most commonly found on my saw is a 1/4" skip tooth blade with 6 teeth-per-inch. It cuts quickly and smoothly both with and across the grain and, as shown in the drawing, it can cut a radius down to 5/8".

When cutting lengths of stock

longer than a couple of feet, support the off-feeding sections with a roller support. Because the stock droops quickly after leaving the short band saw table, it's necessary to keep the support quite close to the machine (within 1′ to 2′), and adjusted slightly below table level.

When making tight radius cuts, it often helps to first run in relief cuts parallel to the radius of the curves. When the saw blade reaches these radius cuts, the tension on the blade is instantly relieved, allowing it to cool and to reorient itself, if necessary, to the layout line.

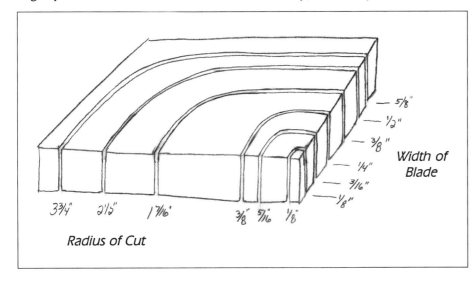

Choosing a band saw blade.

Width of Blade

— 5/8″
— 1/2″
— 3/8″
— 1/4″
— 3/16″
— 1/8″

Radius of Cut

3 3/4″   2 1/2″   1 7/16″   3/8″ 5/16″ 1/8″

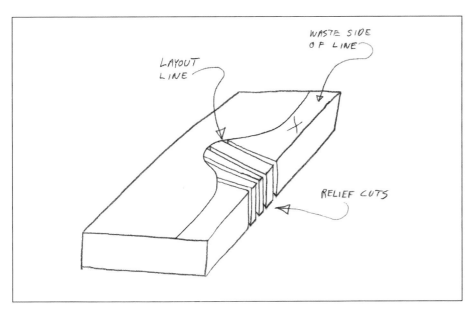

Alleviating binding in small radius cuts using relief cuts.

WASTE SIDE OF LINE

LAYOUT LINE

RELIEF CUTS

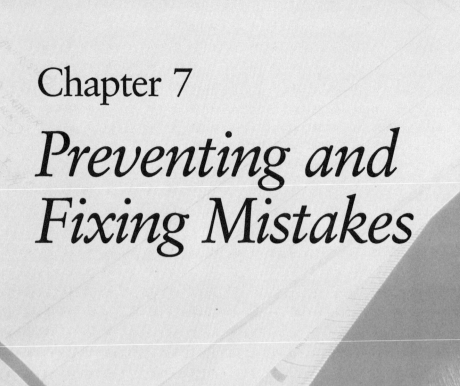

Chapter 7

Preventing and Fixing Mistakes

M istakes happen. At some point, no matter how carefully you try to measure and lay out the cuts, you're going to slip up and make a cut in the wrong place or at the wrong angle. But figuring out how to fix the inevitable miscut is one of the more fun and challenging aspects of woodworking. You can make jigs and alignment tools that may nip these problems in the bud. If necessary, there are ways to recut and rejoin components; there is even a way to "stretch" the width or length of a board. And when all else fails, you can use one of a number of effective techniques to fill or patch defects.

Fit and Alignment Problems

The last thing a woodworker wants to discover after having glued and clamped up an assembly is a miscut joint, a misplaced component or a distorted edge or surface. It is possible, however, to prevent the nightmare of having to fix a permanently joined structure if you take certain precautions. Begin by pre-testing all the joints with a sample of the opposing joint cut into a scrap of wood. Rather than aligning components to a mark, use a temporarily installed strip of wood as an accurate and secure stop. Finally, when gluing the assembly, orient the clamps to keep the structure square. To keep a lamination flat, install moldings between the clamping cauls and the boards to redirect the clamping forces.

Joinery test blocks

When laying out a set of joints (such as the four corners of a mortised-

Before assembling a structure, I test each joint individually, hoping to prevent fitting and alignment problems. Here I am checking the fit of a tenon to a sample mortise that I've carefully cut into a hardwood block.

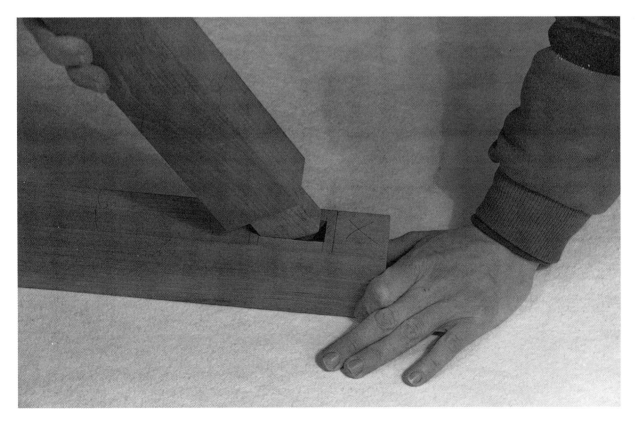

Because I undercut the tenon on this piece of stock, I am building it out by gluing on a piece of veneer. When dry, I'll check and adjust the fit to the mortise in the test block.

Aligning a mortise-and-tenon joint. *If the corner is not square, plane the shoulder of the tenon joint (both sides). If the face of the joint is not flat, plane the shoulder on one side.*

and-tenoned frame), take the time to make a test mortise to verify fit and alignment. Testing and adjusting each joint greatly increases the chance of the assembled structure going together without a hitch.

Make the test block from a hardwood scrap about 6" long cut to the same thickness as the tenon stock. Be sure that the edge to be joined is perfectly square with either face. Lay out and cut the mortise as precisely as possible.

After cutting all the tenons in the set to the layout lines, try each in the test block to assess fit. If necessary, use a chisel or rabbet plane, paring the tenon until the fit is just snug. If the fit is too loose initially or your paring is overzealous, you can build out the cheeks of the tenon by gluing on a thin veneer of wood and then paring it to fit.

When the fit is right, check the alignment of the joint. With the tenon's shoulders tight to the test block, the piece should be flat and square to the test block. If the joint is not square, change the angle of the shoulder with a rabbet plane. You may have to adjust both sides of the piece. If the joint is not flat, pare down one shoulder to change the face angle.

Alignment sticks

To keep components from shifting away from their marks during assembly, I often index them against

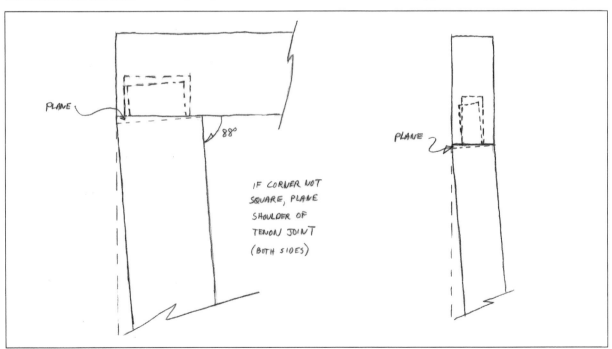

PLANE

88°

IF CORNER NOT
SQUARE, PLANE
SHOULDER OF
TENON JOINT
(BOTH SIDES)

PLANE

scraps of wood fixed temporarily to the structure. I cut the scraps to the length of the spacing layout between the components. Because this length is critical, I mark the dimension on the sticks directly off the full-scale drawing or story pole. Holding the component firmly to the sticks, I fasten and clamp it into place.

In some situations, such as when aligning the spacings of a series of components, I use the story pole itself as an indexing tool. With one end of the components fastened to their marks, I'll temporarily tack a story pole to the free ends to keep them in their proper positions. In the accompanying drawing, the story pole aligns the top front edge of the plywood partitions of a kitchen cabinet unit. With the partitions held firmly and precisely on their marks as indicated on the story pole, the face frame is ready to be attached to their front edge. The pole prevents the partitions from going out of alignment with one another during the fastening process.

Preventing distortion during clamp-up

When a structure is being drawn tightly together with clamps, the

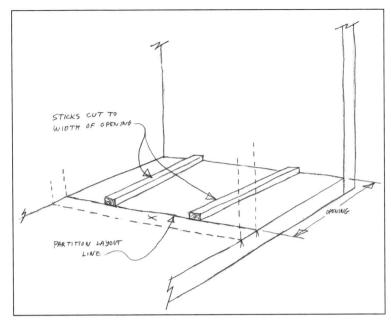

Assembly alignment sticks. *Fix the alignment sticks temporarily in place with double-sided tape.*

Story pole in use as an alignment stick.

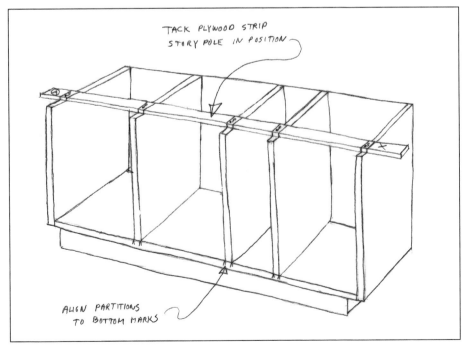

tremendous forces involved sometimes throw the assembly out of square or flat. To prevent problems further down the road, you must be prepared to deal with this before the glue dries.

If you find that the clamps have

pushed an assembly out of square (the measurements from corner to corner are not the same), you can reset the clamps to exert a sideways force. The greater the angle of the clamps, the more sideways force they will exert. If a straightedge reveals that the clamps have bowed the structure, you may be able to force it back to flat by adding more clamps or a heavy weight on the side of the bow. You can help prevent bowing from occurring in the first place by inserting a molding between the clamp pads and the components. Also check to be sure that the clamp bars themselves are flat. Curved bars inevitably produce curved laminations.

Throughout the clamping process, pause regularly to check to see that the joints are flush. Nudge any offending pieces into agreement with a rubber mallet. You might find it necessary to encourage particularly stubborn components to align

During assembly, this face frame pulled itself out of square. I'm pulling it back into square by applying the bar clamps at an angle — they now exert a sideways force as they clamp the structure together.

Redistributing bar clamp forces to resolve a clamping problem. Problem: *Because the clamp cauls do not ride perpendicular to the bars, the forces are not parallel with the wood. As a result, the boards tend to bow upward.* **Solution:** *Inserting half-round molding between the cauls and the boards distributes the forces evenly.*

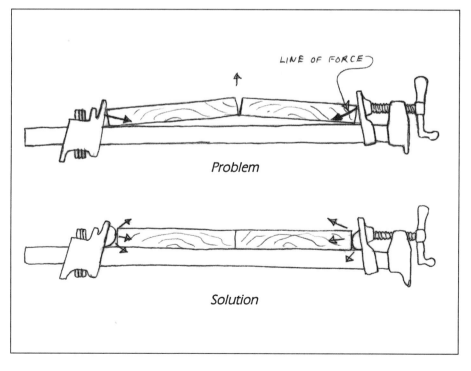

LINE OF FORCE

Problem

Solution

with one another by installing a C-clamp across the joint, or by drawing one piece down to the clamp bar.

Misaligned Components

If the preventative measures outlined previously do not produce a properly aligned and tightly joined structure, you may have to cut the joints again. If the assembly has been glued and set, things are going to get a little ugly (temporarily anyway): This fix is tricky and time-consuming.

The first step is to determine which joint (or joints) is throwing off the structure. Test each joint for squareness and flatness with a combination square. Even a single off-angle corner joint can throw the entire assembly out of square. A miscut length distorts the shape as the components attempt to adjust themselves to the uneven dimensions.

Select the thinnest backsaw in your inventory, remove any metal fasteners that cross the cutline, and

recut the joint. For a miter, align the saw directly on the joint line. If the pieces butt together, crosscut the butting piece as close to the joint as possible. Be careful not to mar the other component.

With a sharp block plane, adjust the recut joint to the correct angle. Remove the least amount of material necessary to true the joint. Be

I use a thin backsaw to recut this misaligned butt—the fine kerf will not significantly throw off the overall dimension of the structure. I cut the butting component as close to the joint as possible.

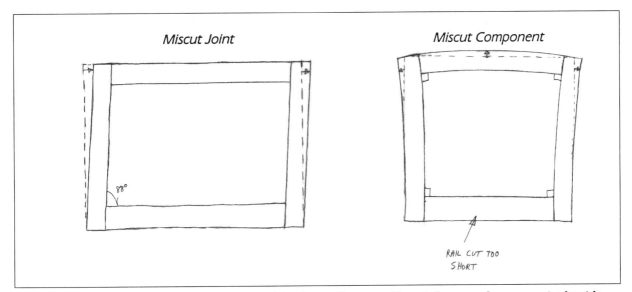

Miscut Joint

88°

Miscut Component

RAIL CUT TOO SHORT

Effects of miscut joints on assemblies. *A miscut joint throws the assembly out of square. A component miscut in length distorts the shape of the assembly.*

This miter joint, before I re-cut it, was joined with a full-length spline. Instead of attempting to recut for a spline, I use a doweling jig to guide drill holes for a dowel joint.

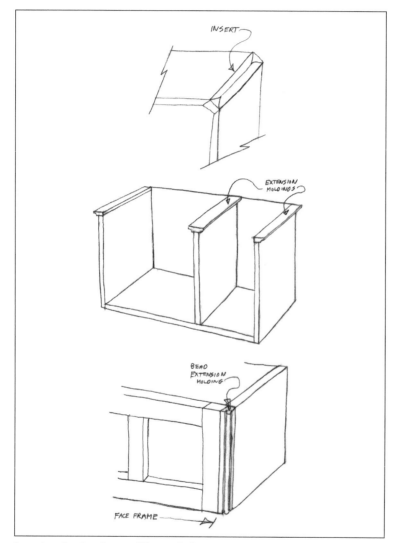

Insert and extension moldings. *An insert molding overlays a corner miter joint, replacing a miscut.*

Extension moldings raise the height of case sides on a partition wall.

An extension corner molding extends the length of a face frame.

careful not to overdo it. You may fix this particular joint, but the short-ened piece (pieces, if a miter joint) can significantly throw off the over-all dimensions of the assembly.

Joint inserts and extension moldings

If recutting and refitting a joint would clearly threaten the overall size of the structure, consider add-ing insert moldings. These are strips of wood, often cut with a decorative profile, placed between the two components at the line of the joint. The inserts allow the components to be cut back and adjusted to fit with-out causing any overall loss of length. To fit the insert, trace its outline over the joint with a knife. Then cut out the area with a fine dovetail saw.

You can also use moldings to ex-tend the size of already assembled structures. If you are careful with their proportions and details, exten-sion moldings can look like they were part of the original design. And they are, if you can keep a secret.

Rejoining the components

After recutting the joints you must rejoin them. Unfortunately, what may have once been a strong and complex joint is now reduced by the recutting process to a simple butt joint. You have two options: Leave the joint a butt and fasten it together as best you can with glue and hidden screws or finish nails (which is fine if it's not used in a load bearing ap-plication), or create some form of mortise-and-tenon joint.

Since it is probably impossible at this point to dismantle the entire structure to re-create the original joint, the simplest way to implement

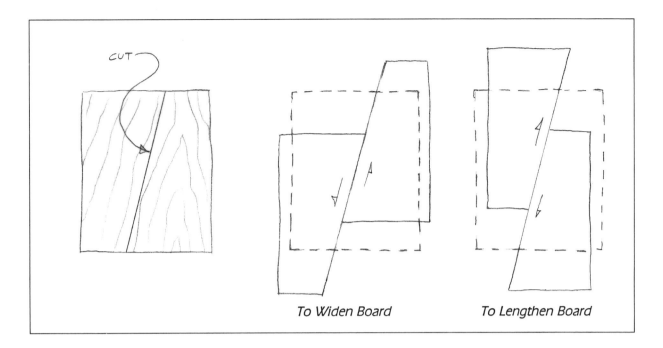

To Widen Board   To Lengthen Board

this last option is to remill the joint for either dowels or spline biscuits. Both of these methods can usually be performed without having to fully remove the components.

"Stretching" Widths and Lengths of Components

While extension moldings can add to the width of an assembly, such a visually obvious solution may not be appropriate in all situations. To discreetly add width, it is sometimes possible to laminate a strip of wood to an edge. To hide the glue line, choose a strip of wood with similar coloration and grain pattern. Also, be sure the joining surfaces are flat and straight. Blend the two pieces with a cabinet scraper followed by fine sandpaper.

Another lamination technique that creates a virtually invisible seam can be used if the stock has not already been cut to length. I once used this trick when confronted with laying out a wide component on a piece of gorgeous material that fell about ½″ under width. To widen the board, I followed this procedure: I first ripped the board diagonally in half, taking care to make the cut along the run of the grain. I then reglued the pieces together, first sliding the halves toward one another until I had the width I needed. Although this shortened the board, I still had the length I needed for this particular component. Because the lamination seam ran parallel to the grain lines, it was impossible to see after scraping and sanding.

You can also use this "slide-by" lamination technique to lengthen a board. After ripping the stock in half diagonally, slide the boards by each other in the opposite direction, away from one another. The board lengthens while becoming narrower.

A good method for lengthening stock that is square or round in cross section is to use one of two varieties of long scarf joints. Don't worry

Slide-by lamination technique. *Rip the board at a diagonal, roughly parallel to the grain. Slide the halves toward each other to widen the board. Slide the halves away from each other to lengthen the board.*

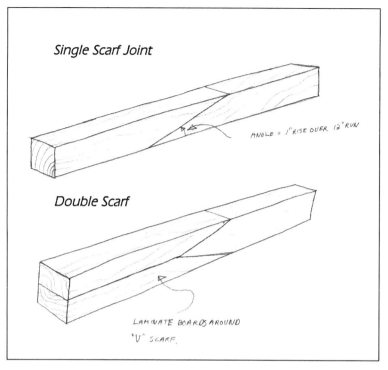

Single Scarf Joint

ANGLE = 1" RISE OVER 12" RUN

Double Scarf

LAMINATE BOARDS AROUND
"V" SCARF.

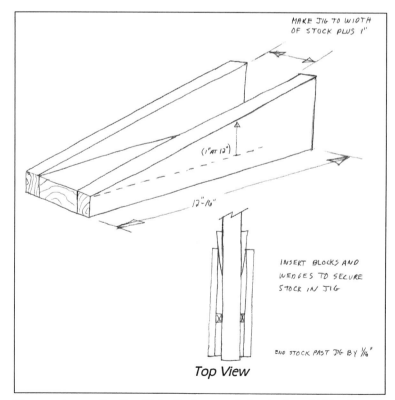

MAKE JIG TO WIDTH
OF STOCK PLUS 1"

(1" AT 12")

12"-16"

INSERT BLOCKS AND
WEDGES TO SECURE
STOCK IN JIG

END STOCK PAST JIG BY 1/16"

Top View

Shop-made scarfing jig. *Make the base and cheeks from ¾" hardwood.*

about losing any strength across this type of joint. Tests show that a well-made scarf joint does not detract from the original strength of the wood. And when done well, a scarf joint is nearly invisible.

I use a shop-made jig to make scarf joints. I design the jig to cut the scarf angle at a 1" rise over a 12" run. This is the most angle a scarf joint needs to maintain full strength. But if strength isn't a primary concern, the angle can be reduced to as low as one in eight.

Lay out the scarf joint on the side of the stock using the angled cheek of the jig. After inserting the wood into the jig, trace the angle along the top edge of the cheek. Remove the stock and cut close to the line with a hand rip saw or band saw. To clean up the cut and make the joint surface perfectly flat, reinsert and clamp the stock securely into the jig. Let the cut extend about ¹⁄₁₆" past the cheeks. Then use a jack plane bridged across the cheeks of the jig to surface the joint. Be careful not to let the plane cut into the cheeks.

After cutting and planing both components smooth and flat, prepare for glue-up and assembly. Because of the slope of the joint, the parts have an enormous tendency to slip by one another. Restrain them with a pair of clamping cauls made from scrap wood cut to the width of the stock. To provide room for the clamps past either end of the joint, make the cauls about 3" longer than the scarf joint.

After applying glue to both joint surfaces, put the pieces together, cover the ends of the joints with wax paper, and then sandwich the assembly between the two clamping

With a piece of stock wedged into my shop-made scarfing jig, I use a jack plane bridged across the cheeks of the jig to true up the rough cut scarf angle. The jig is secured to the bench with screws.

cauls. Then tightly secure C-clamps to either end of the cauls beyond the joint line. This should eliminate any slippage along the joint. Now continue to clamp across the area of the joint itself. Exert just enough pressure to draw the joint tight. If you overdo it, you might squeeze out too much glue, weakening the joint.

Patching Gaps, Holes and Defects With Wood

Several years ago when living on the north coast of California, I built a small bookcase out of second growth redwood for some longtime clients who lived in the desert of southern California. Out the shop door, the project looked great—a client-pleasing design with clean surfaces and tight-fitting joinery. Unfortunately, the clients were not pleased for long. As it says on the bumper sticker (woodworker's version): "Shrink Happens."

The trouble began with my naïveté in building the piece with wood whose moisture content was in equilibrium with the northern California rain forest, or about 12 percent. When the piece acclimated to its new home in a desert with 4 percent to 6 percent ambient moisture levels, the wood loudly announced my blunder by shrinking. Many of the joints opened up, leaving unsightly gaps. To make matters even worse, a couple of knots in the side panels (they looked plenty tight in my shop) loosened and fell out.

To add insult to injury, the pair of gorillas entrusted with delivering the piece from the trucking company's southern warehouse managed to ram it into something when offloading it from the truck. The "scratch" the truckers warned me

about turned out to be a canyon-like rift in one of the corner stiles.

It was not a happy phone call that summoned me to make the trek to the dry lands of the South. But off I went with a bag full of hand tools and a hat full of tricks.

To discreetly close the joint gaps, I brought wedged-shaped pieces of redwood. To replace the missing knots, and to repair the gouged stile, I packed along a stash of redwood stock salvaged from the waste cuts of the project. When I was done, it's likely the patches I left behind might only be found by those who were there to see me make them.

"Wedging" joint gaps

Always make gap-filling wedges from material as close as possible in coloration and grain to the stock surrounding the afflicted joint. Be sure to cut the wedges so that the side grain, rather than the end grain, shows after being driven into place. This makes the wedges nearly invisible.

Because the band saw produces too rough a cut, slice the wedges on a table saw equipped with a fine-

I have filled the gap across this butt joint with wedges made from wood with the same graining and coloration. After I trim and sand the wedge flush to the surface, it will be nearly invisible—a more effective solution than using a filler putty.

Wedges for filling joint gaps. *Always use wedges made with the grain running lengthwise.*

How to cut out wedges. First cut: *Place a blank in the box, edge grain up, wide side toward the blade. Slice through the wood, producing the first wedge.* **Second cut:** *Flip the blank over and cut out the second wedge. Continue to flip and cut until the stock is too small to comfortably hold against the fence.*

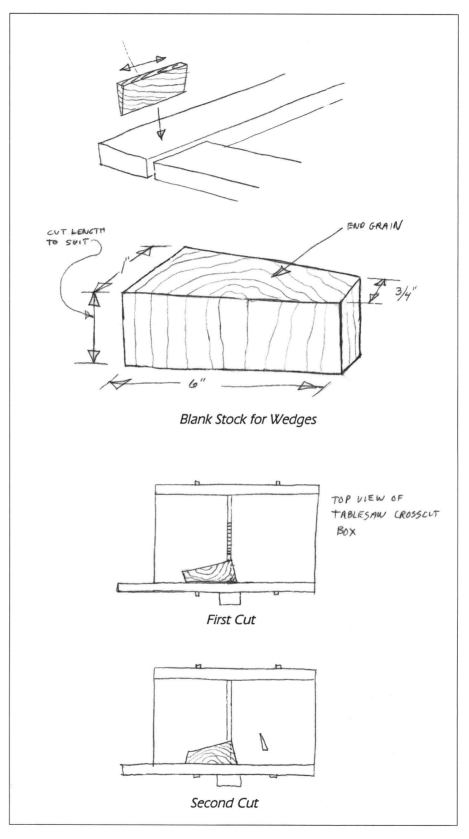

CUT LENGTH TO SUIT

END GRAIN

3/4"

6"

Blank Stock for Wedges

TOP VIEW OF TABLESAW CROSSCUT BOX

First Cut

Second Cut

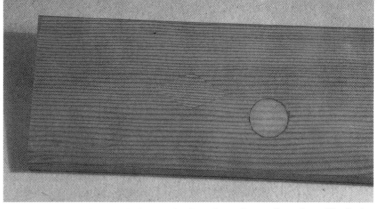

toothed blade. Once armed with a stack of inserts of varying sizes, you can then select the ones that will fill the gap completely before bottoming out. To install them, begin by injecting glue into the gap (a horse syringe from your local vet works great). Then lightly spread glue on each side of the wedge and tap it into place. Tap gently because the grain is running with the length of the wedge, not across it, making it quite fragile. When the glue sets, chisel the wedge down close to the surface and then smooth it flush with a cabinet scraper followed by fine sandpaper.

The "Dutchman's" patch

I have never been able to find out where the term "Dutchman" for an inlayed wooden patch has come from. Perhaps it has something to do with the little Dutch boy who stuck his thumb into the leaking dike. If the end of his thumb was diamond-shaped, that would cinch it for sure. The diamond shape of a Dutchman's patch is one of the features of this type of inlay that helps hide its presence.

More crucial, however, to the success of this fix is the choice of stock from which the patch is made. In the best of all worlds, you would make the Dutchman from a scrap selected from a stash of project offcuts saved just for this purpose. Admittedly, this is wishful thinking if you heat your shop with a wood stove. In any case, the patch needs to be made from stock with as similar coloration and grain pattern to the project as possible.

Begin making a Dutchman by drawing a diamond shape around the area to be repaired. In most situ-

Notice how the diamond shape of a Dutchman's patch makes this fix far less noticeable than that of a circular patch. A Dutchman made from a well-matched piece of wood and oriented with its long dimension running with the grain of the wood can be a nearly invisible repair.

I use a chisel to waste out an inlay mortise for a Dutchman's patch. Note that I have outlined the mortise with a knife cut.

ations, the longer the diamond shape runs in the direction of the wood grain, the more invisible it will be. Trace the diamond onto vellum or Mylar, and then transfer it to a piece of wood ¼″ thick. Slide the diamond pattern around on the stock until the grain pattern of the patch matches that of the wood surrounding the defect. Cut out the patch with a fine saw, and plane a slight (1° to 2°) underbevel on the edges. This underbevel assures a tight fit when the patch is later clamped into place.

Now transfer the shape of the Dutchman to the stock. Hold it tight to the wood over the defect, underbevel side down, as you trace

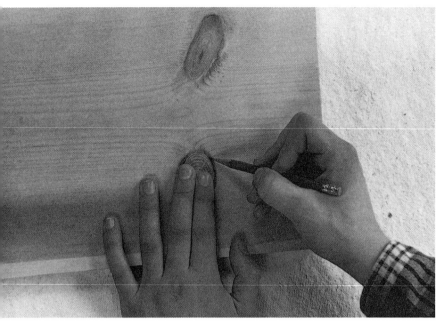

The knot in this piece of paneling has fallen out—I am preparing to replace it by tracing around a slightly larger knot obtained from another board. After opening up the hole to the line with files, I'll glue in the new knot with epoxy.

Commercial filler putties are a good way to go for filling small defects. My favorite filler is the colored clay putty in the small jars at the center of the picture. The putties to either side are hardening putties that work well for larger defects and for surfaces that are to be painted.

around it with a sharp knife. Chisel out the waste between the lines to a depth of about $\frac{3}{16}''$. Dry-fit the patch in the mortise, adjusting as necessary by planing off very fine shavings along the edges (be careful to maintain the underbevel). When you're satisfied with the fit, coat the edges of the patch and the mortise with epoxy and then clamp the Dutchman into place. Distribute the clamping pressure with a wood scrap slightly larger than the patch. When dry, remove the clamp and plane the patch flush to the surface of the wood. Finish up with a cabinet scraper followed by fine sandpaper.

Replacing missing knots

Knowing that even the best made Dutchman's patch is still discernable to the practiced eye, I opt to replace a missing knot with a slightly larger version. I look through my stash of scraps for a likely volunteer. The ideal candidate is a loose knot (indicated by a surrounding thin black ring) sized just slightly larger than the hole in the stock. If the knot doesn't come free with a light tap of a hammer, I throw the wood into an oven heated to about 250° for about half an hour.

I install a replacement knot by first using a sharp, hard pencil to trace its outline around the hole to be filled. I then open up the hole with round files, testing the fit as I approach the pencil line. When I achieve a snug fit, I fix the new knot into place with epoxy.

Patching Gaps and Defects With Filler

For hiding joint gaps too small to fill with wedges, or to fill the irregular cracks that often appear along grain lines or in knots, the best solution is to use a color matched filler material. You can either make your own from a mixture of glue and sanding dust or pigments, or you can choose from a wide variety of commercial fillers.

Among ready-mixed fillers, I have had the most success with the nonhardening clay putties. These fillers are easy to blend together to match any color you want; their smooth texture hides better than the coarser, hardening fillers. Since the clay putties never seem to harden completely, remaining flexible, they are less likely than the hard fillers to fall out when stressed by wood movement.

These nonhardening putties do have a failing, however. If the width of the crack is substantial (over 3/32″), the clay tends to sag over time, creating a shallow depression. For major repairs, choose from the hardening fillers or mix your own hard putty. For filling defects in wood that will be painted, use either a water-based powder filler or a catalyzed mix.

When I first started out in woodworking, one of my mentors showed me his method of making a filler paste from sawdust and glue. After a long hiatus, I recently tried it again, mixing some dust scooped out of my belt sander dust bag with a dollop of carpenter's yellow glue. The results were terrible. When I stained the piece, the coarse-looking patch took on a color three or four times darker than its surroundings.

After exploring some long lost memories, I realized I had probably gone wrong in two ways. First of all, I recalled that in those days yellow

glue was not widely in use, though Elmer's white glue could be found on most woodworker's shelves. A quick experiment showed that sawdust mixed with white glue does not darken nearly as much.

Turning to the coarseness problem, I remembered that my mentor had not just grabbed any old handful of ground-up shavings. Instead, he had sprinkled some incredibly fine dust from a little jar he kept on the shelf. His solution for producing a filler with a smooth texture was obviously in the fineness of the dust he used to make the mix.

Today I use dust collected in the bag attached to my random orbit sander after a session of sanding with fine grit sandpaper (220 or finer). Instead of the white glue, I've gone to transparent glues like five-minute epoxy or cyanoacrylate.

To get a good color match, I skip the dust altogether and tint the glue (usually epoxy) with powdered pigments or acrylic paints I buy at the local art supply store. I use a small, flexible artist's palette knife to work the glue into the defect.

I find that an artist's palette knife is an effective tool for working putty into a crack or nail hole.

Appendix A

Tool Suppliers

Bridge City Tool Works
1104 N.E. 28th Ave.
Portland, OR 97232
(800) 253-3332
Manufactures layout tools of exceptional beauty and precision.

Robert Kahne
511 W. 11th St.
Port Angeles, WA 98362
(206) 452-2292
Dealer of antique hand tools—his brochure usually lists a good stock of Stanley Co. measurement tools.

L.S. Starrett Co.
Athol, MA 01331
Manufacturer of precision measuring and layout tools—the industry's standard.

Veritas Tools, Inc.
12 E. River St.
Ogdensburg, NY 13669
(315) 393-1967
Makers of hooked rules, in addition to a number of other measurement and layout tools.

Woodworker's Supply of New Mexico, Inc.
5604 Alameda Pl. N.E.
Albuquerque, NM 87113
(800) 645-9797
Supplier of drafting, layout and cutting tools, including router bits and pilot bearings.

Matrix Enterprises, Inc.
5926 Sedgwick Rd.
W. Worthington, OH 43235
(614) 846-0030
Maker of Mitermate saw protractor.

The Japan Woodworker
1731 Clement Ave.
Alameda, CA 94501
(800) 537-7820
Carries an extensive line of Japanese hand tools.

Robert Larson Co., Inc.
33 Dorman Ave.
San Francisco, CA 94124
(800) 356-2195
Supplier of a wide range of hand tools.

Appendix B

Further Reading

Drawing and Design

Ching, Frank. *Architectural Graphics*. New York: Van Nostrand Reinhold Co., 1975.

Doczi, Gyorgy. *The Power of Limits*. Boulder: Shambala Press, 1981.

Lawlor, Robert. *Sacred Geometry*. New York: The Crossroad Publishing Co., 1982.

Ramsey, Charles, and Harold Sleeper. *Architectural Graphic Standards*. New York: John Wiley and Sons, Inc., 1981.

Stem, Seth. *Designing Furniture*. Newtown, CT: The Taunton Press Inc., 1989.

Layout Procedures, Jigs and Fixtures

Blandford, Percy. *The Woodworker's Shop*. Blue Ridge Summit, PA: Tab Books, 1989.

Joyce, Ernest. *Encyclopedia of Furniture Making*. New York: Sterling Publishing Co., 1989.

McIntosh, David "Bud". *How to Build a Wooden Boat*. Brooklin, ME: WoodenBoat Publications, Inc., 1987.

Schiff, David, and Kenneth Burton. *Jigs, Fixtures and Setups*. Emmaus, PA: The Rodale Press, 1992.

Toplin, Jim. *Working at Woodworking*. Newtown, CT: The Taunton Press Inc., 1990.

Setting Up and Adjusting Woodworking Machinery

Duginske, Mark. *Mastering Woodworking Machines*. Newtown, CT: The Taunton Press Inc., 1992.

Fine Woodworking on Woodworking Machines. Newtown, CT: The Taunton Press Inc., 1985.

Index

METRIC CONVERSION CHART

TO CONVERT	TO	MULTIPLY BY
Inches	Centimeters	2.54
Centimeters	Inches	0.4
Feet	Centimeters	30.5
Centimeters	Feet	0.03
Yards	Meters	0.9
Meters	Yards	1.1
Sq. Inches	Sq. Centimeters	6.45
Sq. Centimeters	Sq. Inches	0.16
Sq. Feet	Sq. Meters	0.09
Sq. Meters	Sq. Feet	10.8
Sq. Yards	Sq. Meters	0.8
Sq. Meters	Sq. Yards	1.2
Pounds	Kilograms	0.45
Kilograms	Pounds	2.2
Ounces	Grams	28.4
Grams	Ounces	0.04